HURRICANE
CAMILLE

HURRICANE
CAMILLE

Monster Storm of the Gulf Coast

—⦵⦵⦵—

Philip D. Hearn

University Press of Mississippi / *Jackson*

www.upress.state.ms.us

Designed by Todd Lape

The University Press of Mississippi is a member
of the Association of American University Presses.

Copyright © 2004 by University Press of Mississippi
All rights reserved
Manufactured in the United States of America

∞

Library of Congress Cataloging-in-Publication-Data

Hearn, Philip D.
Hurricane Camille : monster storm of the Gulf Coast / Philip D. Hearn.
p. cm.
Includes bibliographical references and index.
ISBN 1-57806-655-7 (cloth : alk. paper)
1. Hurricane Camille, 1969. 2. Gulf Coast (Miss.)—History—20th century.
3. Gulf Coast (Miss.)—Biography. I. Title.
F347.G9H43 2004

363.34'922'09762—dc22   2003025590

British Library Cataloging-in-Publication Data available

This book is dedicated to the memory of my late
father and mother,
Robert B. Hearn and Irma E. McWaters Hearn
of Laurel, Mississippi, whose loving guidance and
support were always there for me;

to my brother, Fred Hearn, my sister, Bobbie Patterson,
and my late sister, Gay Laurendine;

to my darling daughter, Kathy Michelle Hearn;
and to my beautiful wife, Brenda K. Jeansonne Hearn.

CONTENTS

PREFACE AND ACKNOWLEDGMENTS

When Hurricane Camille roared out of the Gulf of Mexico on August 17, 1969, and slammed into Mississippi's 26-mile coastline—with its fashionable beachfront homes, hotels, marinas, lounges, restaurants, and souvenir shops—it left a wake of death and destruction unusual in North American history. Winds clocked at more than 200 miles an hour, a tidal surge of nearly 35 feet, and a barometric pressure of 26.84 inches combined to produce an American nightmare of broken businesses, broken homes, broken lives, and broken dreams. Property damage exceeded $11 billion. The toll in human lives in Mississippi alone reached 172, including 131 dead and 41 missing. But that was just half of the story. The national toll of dead and missing reached 347 as the storm moved through portions of Tennessee and Kentucky, then sparked landslides and flash flooding in West

Virginia and Virginia before finally exiting into the Atlantic and dying quietly off the coast of Newfoundland on August 22. It was one of only three Category 5 hurricanes to hit the U.S. mainland in modern history. The other monsters were Hurricane Andrew, which cut a devastating swath across south Florida in 1992, and the 1935 Labor Day hurricane that hit the Florida Keys. Even the Galveston, Texas, hurricane of 1900—the deadliest in U.S. history, with more than 6,000 killed and missing—was just a Category 4.

Today, the vacant lots, slabs, steps, and driveways leading to nowhere are still visible along the Mississippi Coast, where many older residents date events as BC and AC—before Camille and after Camille. The ruins, however, are largely overshadowed these days by the dazzling lights and bustle of a dozen casinos and companion highrise hotels dominating the beachfront horizon that was, in times past, more serenely characterized by rambling homes, family restaurants, dim motels, and schooner sails. The busy traffic flow and flourishing economy that define the Coast in the new century may be traced to the state's legalization of gambling in 1991. The lure of the slots and gaming tables created a magnet for tourists, sparked a construction boom, and pumped badly needed tax dollars into state and local governments. For the Coast, these are the best of times. New U.S. census figures show that nearly 90,000 people, pursuing warm climate, job opportunities, and southern hospitality, moved into Mississippi's three coastal counties and the three adjacent counties immediately north between 1995 and 2000. The contrast between 1969 and today is stark—but traces of Camille provide a lingering reminder of what happened more than three decades ago and could happen again.

History, at its most basic level, is about people. At no time is that more apparent than in a time of natural disaster when the lives of individuals are snuffed out or forever altered by forces over which they have no control. Ordinary people going about their daily routines one day are suddenly and tragically caught up in a life-and-death struggle the next. Some survive and others do not. Some live to tell the tale, and the dead become a part of the toll, the disaster's grisly body count. This book focuses on some of the survivors of Hurricane Camille—what they were doing in the days and hours of that fateful August weekend before all hell broke loose, their harrowing ordeals during the storm, and their plight and actions in the aftermath. In many cases, they watched family and friends disappear in the dark, debris-filled waters as one of the most powerful storms in U.S. history aimed its fury at the Mississippi Gulf Coast. Their painfully compelling individual accounts provide a human voice for the story of Camille. The book also paints a broader picture of death and destruction as we follow Camille north and east on a lethal journey through several other states, and it chronicles the recovery efforts of those amazingly resilient Mississippi Gulf Coast residents who, battered but unbroken, bounced back to overcome their worst nightmare, personifying the human spirit at its best.

The summer of 1969 was one for the history books. It was the summer of the Apollo moon landing, the Charles Manson murders in Los Angeles, Ted Kennedy's tragic accident at Chappaquiddick, the acceleration of America's withdrawal from Vietnam, and Hurricane Camille. Johnny Cash's "A Boy Named Sue" and the Rolling Stones's "Honky Tonk Women" filled radio airwaves across the nation, while such movies as *Easy Rider*, *Midnight Cowboy*, and John Wayne's *True Grit* raked in big money at the box office. When the eye of Camille passed through Pass Christian, Mississippi, on the Sunday evening of August 17, I was working the night desk of the United Press International news bureau in Birmingham, Alabama. From that distance, it was difficult to fully comprehend the true extent of what was happening to thousands of trapped individuals on the Gulf Coast. Although I would be transferred back to UPI's Jackson, Mississippi, bureau that fall—later covering the Pearl River flood and Hurricane Frederic, both in 1979—the regrets of an eager 25-year-old reporter who had missed out on covering Camille, one of the biggest stories in Mississippi history, lingered long afterwards. As I drove to the Coast to cover the approaching Frederic a decade later, I wondered what it must have been like to have been caught up in such a powerful storm as Camille. The memories of the ordeal certainly were still fresh in the minds of many Gulf Coast residents, whose cars and trucks filled the northbound lanes of U.S. Highway 49 ahead of Frederic that September day.

It would be another decade after Frederic, in 1989, while serving as news director for the public relations office at the University of Southern Mississippi, that I would discover the riveting interviews with Camille survivors compiled by USM's Mississippi Oral History Program, known today as the Center for Oral History and Cultural Heritage. Reid Derr, interim director of the program at the time, provided valuable assistance. Since its establishment in 1971, the program has recorded approximately 1,200 interviews covering various aspects of Mississippi's recent past: politics and government, organized labor, civil rights, ethnic history, agriculture, journalism, art, athletics, natural disasters, and general culture. The interviews are neither public relations–oriented nor journalistic but are historical in nature. They constitute oral memoirs intended to supplement traditional written sources. The program's purpose is twofold: to preserve local and state history through the designing of oral history projects and the conducting and transcribing of interviews and to help historical societies, corporations, institutions, students, and private individuals preserve their own local history and heritage.

A debt of gratitude is owed to R. Wayne Pyle, former assistant director of the program, for his fine work in conducting the Camille survivor interviews, which are on file in the university's McCain Library and Archives. Pyle recorded 41 Camille interviews between August 14, 1979, and May 2, 1980, in an effort to preserve for future generations the experiences, observations, and reactions of survivors. From those interviews, the oral history program compiled 33 bound oral histories and one written memoir. Every bound volume includes a detailed table of contents, a brief biography of each interviewee, and a finished transcript of the interview. In addition, the interview tapes, editorial drafts, and other supporting materials are available for inspection in accordance with McCain Library and Archives policies. The bound volumes reside in the Cleanth Brooks Reading Room (Room 305) and are available for scholarly use. Further information about the library or specific collections may be obtained by writing McCain Library and Archives, University of Southern Mississippi, Southern Station Box 5148, Hattiesburg, MS 39406, or by calling general information at (601) 266-4345 or archives and manuscripts at (601) 266-4348.

As a former newspaper reporter and editor, I felt compelled to try to make some of those Camille life-and-death experiences known to a wider public audience. Mississippi Gulf Coast Community College historian Charles Sullivan had done a wonderful job telling the story of Camille as a key chapter of his 1986 book *Hurricanes of the Mississippi Gulf Coast.* He touched on some of the survivor stories in that work. But as I read through the USM oral histories in detail, one by one, I realized that those personal accounts painted a human face on the Camille experience. They needed fuller treatment in order to put the terror of the hurricane into proper perspective, from the ringside seat of those who lived through that terror.

Looking at the 33 transcribed interviews on file, I gradually focused in on 15 subjects whose tales of survival up and down the Coast that night, from Ocean Springs on the east to Waveland on the west, varied widely. They tell of losing family members and friends and of their own personal struggles for life. At historic Trinity Episcopal Church, one man lost 13 of 16 family members, including small children whose bodies washed into an adjacent graveyard and mingled with coffins and corpses regurgitating from newly dug graves. Armed with those dramatic accounts, I initially wrote a series of articles that were published in Mississippi newspapers in 1989, 1994, and 1999 to coincide with the 20th, 25th, and 30th anniversaries of Camille. In 2000, Seetha Srinivasan, director of University Press of Mississippi, approached Dr. Charles Bolton, professor and chair of the history department at the University of Southern Mississippi, about the possibility of producing a book on Camille based on the university's oral histories. Dr. Bolton recommended me for the job, and I could not refuse the challenge.

The story of Camille came to life as I pored through the volumes of transcribed tapes of the survivor interviews, taking detailed notes and accumulating piles of notecards on each interview subject before I could begin the actual writing process. As I wrote, I relied heavily on the scholarly expertise of Dr. Bolton, codirector of the center, who provided guidance at every step along the way. Taking time from his busy schedule, he read the drafts of each chapter of the evolving manuscript, reviewed my sources, and made invaluable editing suggestions. I owe a debt of gratitude to Seetha Srinivasan, who patiently guided me through the intricacies of manuscript preparation and publication while providing steady encouragement to a first-time author. I also extend thanks to my University Press editor, Anne Stascavage, a Gulf Coast teenager at the time of Camille, who immediately revealed a close affinity with the content of the book and offered many helpful suggestions as I revised and refined the text. Finally, I am grateful for the sharp eye of copy editor Carol Cox, whose fine work was invaluable in polishing the manuscript for publication.

Over the years, I read every Camille-related newspaper account that I could find, looking for new information and, whenever possible, clipping obituaries to document the deaths of some of the key subjects of the oral history interviews. Among those who had passed on were veteran Harrison County civil defense director Wade Guice, who died of cancer in 1996. In 2003, as part of the research for this book, I interviewed Wade's widow, Julia, who retired from civil defense work in 1982 and who has spent much time and effort in the ensuing years documenting Camille's official toll of dead and missing. She was kind enough to invite me into her 100-year-old home, located just off the beach near the old Biloxi Lighthouse, and to share information she had collected through careful research.

Newspaper accounts in the immediate aftermath of Camille and continuing through the following decades up to the present time played an important role in helping me tie up the many loose ends that are bound to follow in the wake of such a large natural disaster. The thorough and well-written newspaper reports of longtime Biloxi *Sun Herald* writer Kat Bergeron surfaced frequently in the research process, often helping me plug important gaps in the story of the Gulf Coast's physical and emotional recovery, which are a part of Camille's legacy. Published accounts based on interviews of hurricane survivor Ben Duckworth, written by veteran Mississippi newspaper columnist Danny McKenzie and editor-publisher Wyatt Emmerich, also proved valuable in helping me piece together the real story of what happened at the Richelieu Manor apartments in the hours before and during the height of the storm, which demolished the three-story structure and killed eight of its residents. One fact that became crystal clear in the multiple newspaper accounts of interviews with Duckworth—and from an e-mail message I received from another Richelieu survivor, Richard Keller, whose wife, Luane, perished in the carnage—was that no hurricane party took place at the apartment building before or during Camille. I am delighted to help dispel the myth of such a party, which was perpetuated almost single-handedly by another often-interviewed Richelieu survivor, Mary Ann Gerlach. Those frequently cited but inaccurate reports, which sometimes made it appear that Gerlach was the apartment complex's only survivor, have caused much grief and frustration for other Richelieu survivors, many of whom toiled for hours to help secure the building and personal property in advance of Camille's onslaught, then huddled together in terror and prayer as the storm landed during the night.

Among others who helped me along the way were Mary Hamilton, a former faculty member at USM's Cook Library, who directed me to important sources of information during the early stages of my research; USM archivist Yvonne Arnold, who graciously took the time to steer me to Hurricane Camille photo archives on file at McCain Library and Archives and assisted me in gaining clearance for their use; and Jennifer Watson, a member of the USM public relations staff, who unselfishly helped me copy those archival photos to computer disks for eventual reproduction in the book. A special thanks also to Mississippi Gulf Coast photographers Bob Hubbard and Fred Hutchings, whose riveting Camille photographs, some taken before the storm and many depicting the destruction, provide dramatic visual documentation in support of the text, and to the *Sun Herald* for opening its Camille photo archives to me. I would like to thank Betty Hinman of Gulfport for the use of several dramatic photographs taken by her late husband, Chauncey, before and after Camille. My thanks also to Murella H. Powell, local history and genealogy librarian, Harrison County Library System, for her assistance in securing the Hinman photographs for publication.

I must mention two former bosses who played important roles in my career development over the years: former longtime USM public relations director W. E. "Bud" Kirkpatrick of Hattiesburg, a mentor and friend whose professionalism on the job was exceeded only by his genuine compassion for others, and the late Andy Reese of Jackson, for many years the Mississippi news manager for United Press International, a patient and thorough journalist who taught me how to write quickly and accurately under pressure, skills that were fully tested in the writing of this book.

Finally, I would like to thank my long-suffering wife, Bren, who picked up the slack at home on those countless evenings and weekends over a three-year period when I was tied to the computer or sorting through stacks of note cards, file folders, books, newspaper clippings, and diskettes in pursuit of my next paragraph. Despite major health problems for both of us and the loss of close family members during the research and writing of this book about Camille—as well as my departure from USM after more than 18 years there to pursue new career challenges at Mississippi State University—Bren's love and support never wavered.

HURRICANE
CAMILLE

"YOU COULD SEE THE BLACK COMING IN"

Wade Guice decided it was time to activate the Emergency Operations Center at Gulfport, Mississippi. The veteran Harrison County civil defense director issued orders for an increased state of readiness—routine procedure when a storm enters the Gulf of Mexico. That triggered a series of preparatory actions that included manning the Emergency Operations Center on a limited basis, touching base with support agencies such as the Red Cross, checking food and water sources, and preparing a list of storm shelters for publication in the local newspaper. According to Guice, "It was time to top off all the fuel tanks and do our hurricane plans, prepare to cancel leaves . . . check inventories . . . just gear up, tighten up to spring into action in the event we had to evacuate."

It was Friday, August 15, 1969, and for most folks along the scenic Mississippi Gulf Coast between New Orleans and Mobile, Alabama—including those in a 26-mile stretch of homes and businesses lining the sandy beach-front from St. Louis Bay to Biloxi Bay—it was business as usual. After all, most longtime residents of the area had weathered many assaults of wind and water from the murky Mississippi Sound over the years, including the big storm of 1947 and Hurricane Betsy in 1965—both of which had been Category 3 hurricanes on the Saffir-Simpson scale of intensity. No big deal. You just hunker down and ride them out. And coastal newcomers, of course, had no inclination to fear something they had never experienced.

Guice, a former real estate and insurance business-man, and Julia, his wife of 21 years, had nurtured and guided civil defense operations in Harrison County since 1961—Julia as CD director for the city of Biloxi and Wade as director for the county. Julia's earlier volunteer civil defense work had led to Wade's involvement. They were concerned, but confident. They had gone to school on Betsy four years earlier and had significantly tightened up CD operations since that time. As a matter of fact, new and eagerly awaited radio equipment was scheduled to be installed at the Biloxi center the very next day. It was sitting there, but Julia had not had a chance to check it out. A state of readiness usually meant a potential storm was at least three days away from landfall, and might or might not emerge as a threat to the area. Since it was a Friday, however, the Guices worked rapidly in their separate locations to alert the public on the final business day of the week, before residents dispersed to homes across Mississippi's three coastal counties—Harrison, Hancock, and Jackson—and a myriad of weekend pursuits. They would brief local elected officials Saturday morning and keep a close eye on weather developments.

It was a hot August in Mississippi but an even hotter one in western and north-central Africa, where a protracted dry spell sent unusually hot air drifting upward across the Sahara Desert in a westerly direction toward the Atlantic Ocean. It collided with cooler coastal air over the Gulf of Guinea, creating an upper-atmospheric disturbance that was detected as a tropical wave by satellite photographs on August 5. Within four days, by August 9, the storm front was dumping heavy rains on the Leeward Islands as it moved into warm waters south of Cuba.

Back on the Mississippi Coast, U.S. Airman Gregory Durrschmidt, stationed at local Keesler Air Force Base, was enjoying his final weeks of the "slow and easy southern lifestyle of Biloxi" while awaiting anticipated transfer orders to Vietnam, where America was mired in war. "The girls at the Fiesta Club will just have to do without us tonight," Durrschmidt wrote in a daily journal he maintained as he and a few friends packed camping supplies, drinks, and snacks and caught the early ferry for Ship Island—one of several barrier islands located about 10 miles off the coast—and a "weekend of sun, surf and suds."

The weather that weekend of August 9 was still hot and clear on the Mississippi Coast, perfect for an outing.

By that time, however, Air Force and Navy reconnaissance aircraft, hurricane hunters, already were making regular forays into the strengthening disturbance off Cuba, measuring the storm's diminishing air pressure and escalating winds. On the afternoon of Thursday, August 14, a brand-new Category 1 hurricane was officially born in the North Atlantic. It was named Camille. Advisory No. 1 was issued by Dr. Robert H. Simpson, director of the National Hurricane Center in Miami, who said the new storm was "expected to move on a curving path to the northwest, reaching the vicinity of the west tip of Cuba early Friday morning. Conditions favor rapid intensification of this young storm." The storm rapidly intensified into a Category 3 hurricane and pounded western Cuba that Friday evening with 115-mile-per-hour winds and 10 inches of rain. The area's tobacco harvest was destroyed, the sugarcane crop heavily damaged, and three people were killed. Camille was just getting warmed up.

Camille's forward movement stalled briefly from 15 to 10 miles per hour as it passed Cuba and entered the Gulf of Mexico. Then, reinvigorated by the warm, moist air, its tightly wound, eight-mile-wide eye focused sinisterly on the U.S. mainland.

"The heat and humidity are unbelievable this week," Durrschmidt wrote, describing sleepless nights at his Keesler dormitory, where he was "sticking to wet sheets, staring at the ceiling and praying for wind." He noted the increased activity by base aircraft, and surmised that there "must be a storm out there somewhere." He was right. Wind and water were on the way.

On Saturday, August 16, a hurricane watch was issued for the Gulf Coast, extending eastward from Biloxi to St. Marks, Florida, with weather forecasters predicting that the storm would take a northerly turn as it rounded Cuba. Wade Guice, nicknamed "Hard Times" as a youngster growing up in Depression-era Mississippi, stepped up his preparations. After briefing local officials and designating shelter managers, he asked grocery stores, lumber yards, and other retail outlets to stand by for possible Sunday business. Guice believed that the media were his best warning system, and he maintained a good relationship with coast newspapers and broadcast outlets as an effective method of keeping the public informed. At that point, it still looked as though the storm might veer toward Mobile or farther east. Nevertheless, commanders of more than 1,100 Mississippi Army National Guardsmen of the 890th Engineer Battalion and 138th Transportation Battalion—holding regularly scheduled drills that weekend on the Coast and at other sites in south Mississippi's Piney Woods—began monitoring the storm's progress. Active military authorities at Keesler and the Naval Construction Battalion (Seabees) Center in Gulfport also braced for potential trouble.

Pass Christian native Gerald Peralta had just retired from a 20-year Air Force career in July and was newly installed as his hometown's chief of police. He drove to Gulfport about 7 o'clock that Saturday evening to pick up his wife's parents, who were returning to the Coast from a trip to St. Louis. "You could tell something was going to happen," he would remember. "It was—I just can't describe it to you—it was a quiet, still 'something's coming' night." The 38-year-old officer was more perceptive than he realized. Camille's northerly turn never came. Instead, Camille locked on a northwesterly course toward landfall. On this course, it would eventually aim its deadly eye and the lethal punch of its right-front quadrant directly at St. Louis Bay and the city of Pass Christian on the western third of the Mississippi coastline. The state's other coastal cities, however—including Waveland, Bay St. Louis, Long Beach, Gulfport, Biloxi, D'Iberville, Ocean Springs, Gautier, and Pascagoula—also would feel the wrath of the killer storm, in varying degrees of death and destruction.

By that August, the summer of 1969 already was one for the history books. The American death toll from the war in Vietnam had reached 34,000, and a new U.S. president, Richard M. Nixon, was trying to fulfill his campaign promise to find peace with honor. Protests against the war were escalating nationwide and Nixon had begun withdrawing U.S. troops from the quagmire in Southeast Asia. CBS-TV cancelled the popular but controversial *Smothers Brothers Comedy Hour*, Judy Garland died of a drug overdose, and gimpy-kneed "Broadway" Joe Namath announced he was quitting professional football. On July 18, Senator Edward Kennedy walked away from the fatal automobile accident at Chappaquiddick,

Massachusetts, which had claimed the life of Mary Jo Kopechne and short-circuited Kennedy's presidential aspirations. Just two days later, U.S. astronauts Neil Armstrong and Edwin Aldrin took mankind's first walk on the moon to cap the successful Apollo 11 lunar mission. Mississippi's African-American population received welcome news August 8 when a federal appeals court opened use of Mississippi's sandy beaches—previously the domain of whites only—to members of all races. Out west on August 9, police were investigating the deaths of Los Angeles actress Sharon Tate and four others who were ritualistically murdered by followers of Charles Manson. It was a summer of miniskirts, bell-bottoms, eight-track tapes, marijuana, and shoulder-length hair and Afros for men. On August 1, college kids, hippies, music lovers, and others began camping out at Bethel, New York, in anticipation of the Woodstock Music and Art Festival scheduled for the weekend of August 15–18. Top 40 radio stations were blaring out the Rolling Stones's "Honky Tonk Women" and such other hit tunes as Johnny Cash's "A Boy Named Sue," Elvis Presley's "Suspicious Minds," the Beatles's "Here Comes the Sun," and "This Magic Moment" by Jay and the Americans. Movie theaters across the country were attracting big crowds with such box-office hits as *The Wild Bunch, Midnight Cowboy, Easy Rider, Butch Cassidy and the Sundance Kid, True Grit, Alice's Restaurant,* and Walt Disney's *The Love Bug.* Some older film favorites also were still popular big-screen reruns that summer of 1969. Ironically, the beachfront Moonlite Drive-in theater in Pass Christian had booked a special coming attraction for Wednesday, August 21: *Gone with the Wind.* By then, the Mississippi Gulf Coast would be.

Dr. Henry Maggio was living the good life. The 33-year-old physician had a successful general practice in Bay St. Louis and a stylish, 100-year-old home at nearby Waveland, which he shared with his wife, Bobbie, and their three children. With only five medical practitioners in Bay St. Louis, a quaint community known as Shieldsboro in earlier times, Maggio found himself on call that weekend along with another physician, Dr. Marion Dodson. He worked in his office and made his usual rounds Saturday morning, then spent most of the afternoon and night at the Bay St. Louis hospital. He performed surgery on a woman who had suffered a severe hand wound, not finishing his work until about 3 a.m. Sunday. Later he remembered leaving the hospital and driving home along the beach in the predawn hours. "It was a gorgeous night. The stars were clear and everything was fine." When he returned to the hospital about 9 a.m., however, it was filling up with elderly and disabled people who were being transported there from local residences and care facilities. It was "because of the storm," hospital officials told him. "It dawned on me and I asked, 'What storm?'. . . At that time, [I thought] it was still going to hit Pensacola [Florida] or Mobile," he recalled. Quickly, reality set in. Maggio returned to his home, packed his family off to stay with a close friend farther inland at Picayune, closed the storm windows of his home, and returned to the hospital for further duty.

In Gulfport, 1969 had been a terrible year for local attorney Robert L. Taylor, a 40-year-old Tulane University law school graduate and Air Force veteran of the war in Korea. His wife, Beverly Ann, had died of cancer in May, right after they had redecorated their home, which had been heavily damaged by a fire. Then, to make matters worse, Taylor had torn the cartilage in one of his knees while barbecuing chicken. "I was, of course, just beside myself, mentally, physically and financially" that summer of '69, he said. Just back from a business trip to Pensacola that Saturday afternoon, August 16, he stopped by the small craft harbor on the Gulfport beach to check on his beautiful 34-foot racing sloop, *Morgan 34*. He discovered that some of the other local sailors were moving their boats eastward around Biloxi to the back bay area for safer mooring. The city of Biloxi is located on a peninsula, fronting the Gulf to the south and Biloxi Bay on its eastern and northern sides. Taylor and a few others decided they would wait until Sunday morning to move their vessels. Why hurry?

Lois Toomer and her husband, Donald, were in the planning stages for a belated 35th wedding anniversary celebration at their beachfront home in Gulfport. Known in the city for many years as the creative owner of Toomer's Bride Shop on 25th Avenue, Mrs. Toomer, a native of Meridian, was 56 years old. She and Donald, a longtime engineer with Mississippi Power Company, went shopping Saturday for invitations to send to family and friends who might want to attend their planned anniversary event. Lois had already decided on a party theme: "Come. We are having a big blowout!" The real blowout would come earlier than expected.

Meanwhile, out in the darkness of the night, Camille continued to draw strength from the warm waters of the Gulf. Air Force Captain Frederick J. Foss flew a hurricane hunter into the eight-mile-wide eye of the storm and, according to Sullivan, recalled, "I've never seen it rain harder before or since . . . I could see the sky above and the sea below. It was a classically formed hurricane." John Maines, a reporter for the Jackson *Clarion-Ledger*, set the scene in an article published by Mississippi's largest daily newspaper on August 13, 1989:

> *Conditions were perfect . . . for a killer storm. All of the physics that go into the making of a hurricane are not known. But meteorologists who look back to 1969 say conditions were ripe for what scientists know helps breed killer storms. The summer of 1969 had been extremely warm, heating up the surface waters on the Gulf of Mexico to temperatures in the mid and upper 80s. Heat is the source of a hurricane's energy—so in essence, Camille was running on atmospheric high octane . . . The so-called steering currents allowed Camille to gather steam for two days, then sent it rocketing like a giant bowling ball toward man-made structures on the shore.*

An Air Force WC-130 crew clocked Camille's winds at 160 miles per hour, with a barometric pressure approaching a record low and a forward speed of 14 miles an hour. "The first information we had, the first warning we had on Camille was a 15-foot tide and 150 mile-an-hour wind, which is comparable to the 1947 storm—just a little more severe than the 1965 storm, Betsy," Wade Guice remembered. But Camille, by now, was a deadly Category 5 storm, and would be second only to the Florida Keys Labor Day hurricane of 1935 as the most powerful storm in modern history to hit the U.S. mainland. When astrologer Jean Dixon earlier predicted that Sunday, August 17, 1969, would "begin quietly but become more active in later hours," she wasn't just whistling Dixie. She wasn't thinking about the weather, but had hit the nail on the head. Saturday evening, Gregory Durrschmidt, his brother Chuck, and several buddies ate an evening meal at Baricev's Restaurant, one of the Coast's finest beachfront dining establishments, and enjoyed an evening of live music at the Fiesta Club, the popular singles hot spot on the Biloxi strip. On the way back to Keesler, they heard a radio news report that a "long, hard rain did not dampen youthful spirits at Woodstock," which was scheduled to conclude the following day.

By early Sunday morning, another Air Force reconnaissance plane had measured Camille's barometric pressure at 26.84. The Florida Keys storm of September 2, 1935, had had a barometric reading of 26.35, the world's lowest sea-level pressure ever recorded over land. That was cause enough for alarm, but Camille was still 250 miles south of Mobile with the likely strike area not yet pinpointed. It was too close for comfort, however, and Wade Guice issued a hurricane warning for the Mississippi Gulf Coast at 5 o'clock Sunday morning. For him, the timing was perfect, because "[e]verybody is where they're supposed to be. They're at home. Sunday is an ideal time to have an evacuation." Coast residents awoke that morning to hear radio stations and local WLOX-TV blaring evacuation warnings, and thousands began boarding up their homes for the move to civil defense shelters or headed upstate along the arterial highways. Mrs. Jesse Goff of Pascagoula was killed in a two-car crash at a U.S. Highway 49 intersection in north Gulfport, becoming, in a sense, one of Camille's first Mississippi victims.

Mississippi Army National Guard units already on duty were activated and dispersed to various sites along the Coast from Bay St. Louis to Pascagoula. The guard's two-and-a-half-ton trucks and 29 amphibious LARC vehicles also were posted at points considered particularly vulnerable to flooding. Durrschmidt awoke to a rainy but "peaceful" Sunday morning. The Ship Island ferry was gone from the pier, as were most other vessels normally moored there, and people were boarding up windows at houses and businesses all along the beach. Traffic along Highway 90 (part of the Old Spanish Trail national highway from St. Augustine, Florida, to San

Diego, California) was bustling. "We wonder where everyone is headed," Durrschmidt wrote in his journal.

Soon, Keesler's new commander, Major General Thomas E. Moore, evacuated his aircraft and restricted all military personnel and dependents, including Durrschmidt and his buddies, to base barracks or shelters, where they would ride out the storm in relative safety. Captain James H. Hill, Seabees commander, turned the Gulfport base into a formidable shelter area, utilizing a huge concrete-block warehouse to protect military personnel and dependents from the impending storm. According to historian Charles Sullivan in his 1986 book *Hurricanes of the Mississippi Gulf Coast*, the "approximately 800 Seabees on base fired up auxiliary generators, filled water buffaloes (wheeled water trucks) and checked on the center's eight Marine Corps amtracs."

Robert Taylor was down at the Gulfport small craft harbor by 4:30 that morning, accompanied by his friend Billy Barrett, to take *Morgan 34* around to the back bay. An experienced sailor, he and Barrett hung around the docks to help others get started, and so were among the last to leave, along with fellow sailors Bubba Wallace, William Wallace Weatherly, and Scott Watson. By the time they set sail about 8 a.m., however, it was too late. They got hit by a line of squalls near the lee side of Deer Island and had to turn around and head back to port. "We couldn't get up the storm sails," said Taylor. "We were literally blown around. Billy and I had a heck of a ride coming back and those life preservers felt pretty good at that time." Then, they had problems getting back into the Gulfport harbor. Taylor explained: "There was a power boat coming out as we were going in. He had cleared the mouth of the harbor, maybe 200 feet, and we were a little worried about colliding with him because of the narrow channel and the lack of control that we had and [then] his engine quit. He was immediately blown onto the rocks on East Pier and they jumped off onto the pier, and we watched the boat disintegrate in just minutes, in seconds."

By the time Taylor and his sailing companions made it into the harbor, secured their boats, and stashed electronic equipment in the trunks of their cars for safety, it was approximately 9 to 10 a.m. Winds were gusting at about 60 miles per hour, and there were very few boats left in port. Taylor went home and began making preparations for the storm. He filled his bathtubs with water and stocked up on canned goods, candles, batteries, and a nip or two of medicinal courage—"I made sure I had some bourbon," he said—then settled in for a nap. Later, he would be joined by Barrett and a client-friend, Mary Evelyn Wallace. Afternoon radio reports said Camille's winds had reached a strength of 180 miles per hour.

During the calmer weather early that morning, 41-year-old Alma Anderson drove several elderly members of her family to Mass. The Anderson home on Biloxi beach had been in the family for three generations and was thought by the family to be virtually hurricane-proof. It had just been remodeled. "We had spent a fortune on that house," Alma remembered. "We had new carpeting put all downstairs, new drapes, all repainted downstairs, chandeliers all redone." Alma and her husband, Glennan, had lived in the house for a number of years with Glennan's mother, Althea, and a bachelor uncle, Roy, both in their 70s. Two of Glennan's elderly aunts also resided there, including 80-year-old Maurice Stella Tucei. A niece and nephew, the young children of one of Glennan's brothers, were visiting at the time. Later that morning, as the rain set in and the wind picked up steam, a cousin dropped by the Anderson home and said to Alma, "Well, it looks like it's going to hit." Alma picked up the old folks at church and set about making preparations for the approaching storm, stocking up on supplies and nailing plywood panels over windows. It never occurred to the family to evacuate. "Well, my mother-in-law and the old people wouldn't have left that house for all the tea in China," she remembered. "They had been there all their lives, and they had never had one to hit [with such ferocity] as Camille."

Back in Pass Christian, the 50-year-old beachfront home of 73-year-old Edith Byrd de Vries also had weathered many storms over the years. A native of the Bonnie community north of Biloxi, she had taught school for a while in Louisiana before moving to New York City on September 23, 1926, the same day Gene Tunney decisioned Jack Dempsey for the U.S. heavyweight boxing championship in Philadelphia. She spent the next 29 years in the Big Apple, marrying furniture designer Herman de Vries in 1944 and settling with him back on the Mississippi Coast in 1955. Energetic and active for most of her life, Edith broke her hip in an accidental fall eight weeks before Camille and had been confined to a wheelchair. By this time, Herman was living at the Driftwood Nursing Center in Gulfport; however, their adult daughter, Earle, also lived on the de Vries property, which covered most of a block. As the storm approached, they were joined at the big house, located about 800 feet from the beach, by four members of the Lafollette family, who rented a brick house on the north end of the 1,500-foot-deep de Vries property. "It [Camille's approach] didn't bother us at all," Mrs. de Vries would recollect. "All we did, we brought the outdoor iron furniture in on the porch. The cops told them [the Lafollettes] to come to our house to be safe."

Loud hammering awoke H. J. "Ben" Duckworth, Jr., that Sunday morning at Pass Christian's Richelieu Manor apartments—a three-story, U-shaped structure with two wings stretching toward the beach at Henderson Point, a land mass of less than two square miles on the westernmost tip of the Pass Christian peninsula. Fresh out of Mississippi State University with a business degree, the 24-year-old Duckworth had recently landed a real estate development job with Continental Construction Company in Gulfport and moved into a ground-floor apartment at the Richelieu with roommate Buddy Jones, a Navy medical technician. Ben rolled out of bed, donned a swimsuit under his jeans and went to see if he could help the apartment managers, Merwin Jones, 55, and his wife, Helen, 53, get ready for the coming storm. Duckworth said residents had been reassured by the managers that the building was safe. The Richelieu's bottom floor had been flooded by Hurricane Betsy four years earlier, but the complex had suffered no structural damage. "Besides," said Duckworth, "the black-and-yellow signs designated it as a civil defense shelter and, according to the building plans, there were steel beams."

Richelieu residents Mary Ann Gerlach, a cocktail waitress at a local club, and her sixth husband, Frederick (he was called "Fritz"), a 30-year-old Navy Seabee who moonlighted as a weekend bartender, had worked late Saturday night and into the early morning hours Sunday. Later, they stocked up on food and booze. Hurricanes meant time off from work and, after all, they had been through storms before. The Gerlachs planned to eat and get some rest Sunday afternoon, then maybe have a few drinks later to welcome Camille. The following Tuesday, August 19, would be their second wedding anniversary and they had already exchanged gifts. Mary Ann recalled, "We thought, well, this is going to be like a little vacation. We won't have to work and will be able to have a really good time. I went out and got all kinds of stuff to fix sandwiches and hors d'oeuvres, and a bunch of stuff to drink. The manager and his wife said that it was the safest place to be."

Meanwhile, Camille's fury was mounting. An Air Force plane penetrated the swirling storm early Sunday afternoon, reporting a barometric reading of 26.61 and wind speeds approaching a stupifying 200 miles per hour. The hurricane, with its small eye of about eight miles, measured only 80 miles across—half the size of Betsy, but far more powerful. When the new data reached the National Hurricane Center, Dr. Simpson wondered if he were dealing with a small hurricane or a large tornado. And he warned: "Never before has a populated area been threatened by a storm as extremely dangerous as Camille."

By 3:30 p.m., Camille also was pushing a 24-foot tide with a 10-foot sea on top of that. "Any way you slice it, that's [about] a 35-foot wall of water, unprecedented anywhere in the world," noted Wade Guice. By the time the veteran civil defense director received word of the storm's increasing ferocity, there was bumper-to-bumper traffic leaving the Coast, and Guice's evacuation job was nearly 90 percent complete—except, of course, for those who did not heed the warnings. "I don't recall having any panic problems," Guice said, "except for the poor devils that were caught in their homes in the height of the storm. I'm sure they were quite panicked."

Paul Williams was among those who planned to stay on the Coast, but he didn't want to be trapped in his home. He wanted to find a quiet place, somewhere he and 16 members of his family could ride out the approaching storm in peace and safety. An auditorium adjacent to Pass Christian's historic Trinity Episcopal Church—where Williams had served as caretaker for the past 25 years—seemed like the ideal place for refuge. The church, located on Henderson Point, had weathered 18 hurricanes since its construction in 1849. So Williams told his wife, Myrtle, "Honey, I'd like to be where it's quiet, where there's not too much of a big crowd because I can't rest. We'll go up there and stay in the auditorium over yonder." Williams, the son of an itinerant woodcutter, would be celebrating his 50th birthday in a few days, on August 24—if he managed to live that long. After getting permission from the church rector, the Reverend Durrie Hardin, he moved into the church auditorium Sunday evening with his wife, 11 children, three grandchildren, and one son-in-law. "We took our TV, we took our radio. We took us some food and was in the auditorium." They prepared food in the church kitchen and Williams warned the youngsters, "Y'all found it clean. That's the way I want to leave it." After supper, he took off his hat and shoes and found a quiet corner where he could monitor weather reports on television and the radio. Williams remembered: "A little bit later on, the little children—oh, they was having so much fun—just enjoying themselves. So I said, 'Y'all come here, I want to tell y'all something.' They didn't want to listen, just kept on ripping around and tearing. So I said, 'Hear this! Now, if the water come in here, we will go upstairs.'" Then, they settled in for the evening at the old church.

Meanwhile, Piet Stegenga worked at his civil service job at Keesler Air Force Base until the middle of the afternoon, when his boss told him to go to his home and family in Pass Christian and get ready for Camille. "Peter, the thing to do now is go home," Howard Adams told the 58-year-old, Canadian-born Stegenga, whose parents had emigrated to Canada from Holland. "We've done everything we can do here. Go see about your family. That's the main thing. See about your family and get out."

But Stegenga told his boss, "There is no getting out, Mr. Adams. My wife [Valena, 53 at the time] has been taking care of my mother and them for years. There is no way they are going to get out. I'm going to have to stay with them or drown with them . . . Them people are crippled . . . You can't save crippled people in a storm." John Dambrink, Sr., Stegenga's stepfather, was 84 years old, and relatives said he was "feeble minded." They called him "Pops." Anna Dambrink, Piet's 78-year-old mother, suffered from "arthritis in her spine" and had been "bedridden for two years," utilizing a wheelchair to get around. Piet's stepsister, Elizabeth Dambrink, 46, affectionately known as "Sis," tended to the old couple night and day. She too would stay put, along with her brother, John Dambrink, Jr., known as "Joey." Around 4 p.m., the family gathered at the Dambrink house, which was about a block and a half from the Stegenga house. The Stegenga house was located behind Pass Christian High School, about a block north of Trinity Episcopal Church. A little later, Piet and Joey got into Joey's car and rode down to the beach, where they were shocked by the high tide and lapping waves. "I can't get out there in that water and save no people, as bad as this storm is," Piet told Joey. "I'm going to have to fight for my own life. Everybody is going to be on their own in this storm." Joey wasn't convinced. "You're crazy," he replied. But Piet wasn't crazy. He was right—dead right.

Westward across St. Louis Bay, Dr. Maggio had stayed quite busy at the hospital. He paused occasionally to take note of the latest storm reports, which indicated that the hurricane was not turning north as forecasters had predicted earlier. Suddenly, realizing now that Camille was on a straight line for the Waveland–Bay St. Louis–Pass Christian shoreline, the young physician experienced his first-ever anxiety attack:

> *About 4 o'clock in the afternoon, I was sitting in the doctors' lounge and I experienced what I know now to be a true anxiety reaction. I had butterflies in my stomach and a sense of impending doom and disaster that lasted for about five minutes. A very uncomfortable sensation in that I was shaking inside . . . I couldn't do anything about it, but it subsided. I then began to pay attention to the environment and what happened . . . I happened to hear the sound of wind blowing . . . and it was the sound of a woman outside the window, screaming at the top of her lungs. I had heard that same sound in [Hurricane] Betsy . . . and I hadn't heard it since. When I heard it that day at 4 o'clock, I knew we were in trouble.*

Twenty-six miles east, on the opposite end of the beach, across Biloxi Bay in Ocean Springs, 36-year-old banker John Switzer watched water creep up a draw located behind his Ruskin Avenue home. In Gulfport, Lois Toomer put aside her wedding anniversary party plans and spent the afternoon packing things away, with the help of her longtime maid and friend, Mary Fitzpatrick. As Donald left for storm duty at the utility company's service center, Lois and Mary went to the home of Mrs. Toomer's older sister, just west of Gulfport in Long Beach.

At his Gulfport home just before dusk, Robert Taylor heard a National Guard vehicle drive by, with guardsmen warning residents by way of a loudspeaker to evacuate. But Taylor said he didn't consider leaving, recalling, "I knew the hurricane of '47 (with a 14-foot storm surge) hadn't covered the lot." Just west of Bay St. Louis, Waveland alderman Johnny Longo, a 40-year-old Italian-American from New Orleans, noticed seagulls flying inland in air so thick and muggy he could hardly breathe. "Even then," he said, "it's man's competitive nature and his sense of security that he always feels like, Well, this won't happen to me. I'll stay around and see what happens."

Sullivan captured the mindset of many Mississippi coast residents at the time:

> *Many not only refused to believe the reports, but also scoffed at them. Guardsmen and civil defense workers armed with contour maps went into areas not considered low-lying by coast standards and tried to convince inhabitants that they were facing something beyond imagining.*

*But many people living at 20-foot elevations refused to
believe they were going to get 10 to 15 feet of water above
that. The standard rejoinder was, "I rode out the '47 hurricane and Betsy (in 1965) and I'll ride out this one too . . ."
The prize for that brand of suicidal mentality went to the
denizens of Pass Christian's Richelieu Apartments.*

For some Richelieu residents, like the Gerlachs, the hurricane indeed seemed like an excellent opportunity "to
have a really good time," later, after their nap. For most
others in that doomed complex, however, Sunday was a
day spent working, waiting, and praying.

Ben Duckworth's roommate, Buddy Jones, was called
to Gulfport's Seabee base for duty Sunday, but Duckworth and some other Richelieu residents—such as
Richard Keller, a NASA engineer with General Electric—
spent most of the day helping manager Merwin Jones
nail precut plywood panels across apartment windows
and carrying furniture and other personal belongings
from first-floor units to the third floor of the complex.
They also cleared the Richelieu pool area of patio furniture and helped Pass Christian police move the cars of
several neighborhood residents to higher ground. Duckworth's father telephoned from Jackson that afternoon
and begged his son to leave. "But radio reports said the
escape routes were clogged, so we decided to stay," said
Ben, noting that Merwin Jones had offered the use of a
vacant apartment suite on the third floor to any who
planned to ride out the storm. Also, he said he and sev-

eral of the younger men in the complex had agreed to look after an elderly retired couple who lived in the building, Jack and Zoe Matthews. Keller and his wife, Luane, both from Boston, also decided to stay. Earlier, they had thought about going to a local shelter, but were told their small pet dog would not be admitted. "Luane said she had seen Atlantic storms but had never seen a Gulf Coast storm," Duckworth remembered. "She had decided to stay and cook a roast." The Gerlachs, Mary Ann and Fritz, slept. Duckworth said there were 26 people in the Richelieu when a policeman (probably Peralta) came by about 6 p.m. to get a list of names. At least five of those folks, he said, had evacuated by 7:30 p.m. Most of the Richelieu residents thought the building's frame was made of steel, which had been called for in the original construction plans, said Duckworth, but they would find out much too late that the building's frame "was nothing but wood."

Chief Peralta and his three-man police force spent most of the day trying to get Pass Christian residents, including those at the Richelieu, to evacuate. The chief, once a promising young baseball player, said he went to the Richelieu and made a personal appeal to Merwin Jones "two or three times" during the afternoon. Peralta said he entered through a back gate in the middle of the northern side of the apartment complex and went down a walkway to the open patio area at the pool. He remembered his conversation with the apartment managers:

*I can picture him [Mr. Jones] standing right there talking
to me. He had a drink in his hand, and he wore glasses, and
I made the comment, "Mr. Jones, if this water gets over this
first story, what are you going to do?" He said, "Well, I'm
going up to the third floor because it's three stories." I said,
"Well, if you get up to that third floor and that floor washes
out from underneath you, what are you going to do?" "I
guarantee," he said, "well, I don't think it will get there."
Well, none of us did, you know. It was a three-story building. And he said, "I don't think it will get that bad."*

By 5 p.m., Peralta and his officers were riding the
streets of Pass Christian, going ward to ward, pleading
with residents to get out. At the Richelieu, a traveling
salesman, apparently known by some of the residents,
came by and tried to organize a hurricane party. "We
were too exhausted and when he couldn't find any takers,
he got into his car and headed toward New Orleans,"
Duckworth recalled. "That probably saved his life." Some
of the Richelieu residents watched, mesmerized, from the
building's balcony as the Gulf waters rose steadily over
the sand beach just beyond U.S. 90. Joining Duckworth
and the Kellers in the empty third-floor suite, apartment
316, to ride out the storm were Mike Gannon, a Navy
Seabee just back from Vietnam, and Mike Bielan, a NASA
engineer with North American Rockwell. "There were a
few beers poured," said Rick Keller. "But the group of
people huddled in front of the TV that night while power

lasted were not partying and were doing more praying than anything."

At 6 o'clock, the big siren at the Pass Christian fire station screeched the storm's impending, relentless approach. Peralta drove down to the beach seawall and watched the silhouette of a shrimp boat racing across the Gulf toward shore. "That water was calm, just as calm as it could be," he remembered. "But right behind it, you could see the black coming in."

THE HISTORY OF THE MISSISSIPPI GULF COAST

Humans have inhabited or traversed what is now the Mississippi Gulf Coast for thousands of years. Archaeologists confirm that wandering bands of Native American hunters pursued animals for food in the Biloxi area and on nearby Deer Island as far back as the Paleo-Indian stage, circa 14,000–12,000 B.C.E. Hurricanes may have discouraged the formation of large and permanent villages in the area, but there is ample evidence that archaic people organized into small nomadic groups. The Spanish explorer Hernando de Soto came into contact with survivors of the disappearing Mississippian culture in the early sixteenth century. The ancient Indian inhabitants—the Biloxis, the Pascagoulas, and the Acolapissas—left no written records of the huts and crops that likely suffered hurricane damage both before and after Columbus. The coastal tribes, over time, gradually mixed and mingled with other Native American groups and faded into Mississippi Coast history. The three tribes mentioned above, however, as well as the Capinan Indians, were there when the French arrived in 1699—the beginning of the area's recorded history and, for all practical purposes, the beginning of the end of Native American presence. The French explorers found only the earthen remnants and shell piles of the long-forgotten Paleo, Archaic, Woodland, and Mississippian periods. Artifacts recovered in archaeological digs are all that remain to provide a glimpse of the life and times of those early civilizations. The Biloxis and the Acolapissas were the historic Indian settlements nearest the Gulf, with the former located more than 15 miles north on the Pascagoula River and the latter inhabiting an area farther west, along the Pearl River, about four miles inland. No coastal settlements of any kind existed between those two rivers or anywhere along the Coast during that early period of history.

The body of coastal waters known as the Mississippi Sound is about 80 miles long, extending from Mobile Bay across the entire Mississippi coastline to Lake Borgne in Louisiana. Fairly shallow, the water averages about 10 feet deep and is very muddy. The Sound is fed by three rivers—the Pearl River on the west and the Pascagoula and Alabama rivers on the east. The Jourdan and Wolf rivers empty into St. Louis Bay, located between the cities of Bay St. Louis (earlier called Shieldsboro) on the west and Pass Christian on the east. Also emptying into the back bay of Biloxi are the inland waters of the Biloxi River, the Tchoutacabouffa River, and Bayou Bernard. Those waters reach the Sound through Biloxi Bay, located between Biloxi on the west and Ocean Springs on the east.

About 10 miles off the coast, running parallel to the shoreline, is a string of long, narrow islands called the barrier islands. Mike Hobbs, in "Mississippi's Offshore Islands," wrote this description: "Strung like pearls on a strand off Mississippi's coast, Petit Bois, Horn, East Ship, West Ship, Cat plus Round and Deer Islands are all sites of many fascinating stories and events which shaped the Coast and the country." The islands range from a few to several miles long and about a third of a mile wide, and most are barely visible from the mainland, except for Deer Island—described by Hobbs as "a thin stand of tall pine trees rising up from Biloxi Bay . . . within a half-mile of Biloxi's beachfront." An amusement park constructed on Deer Island in the early twentieth century was blown away by a hurricane in 1915. All of the islands, at one point or another, according to Hobbs, were "trod upon by explorers, fishermen, pirates, colonists, farmers, soldiers and sailors."

To the east and nearest to Mobile lies six-mile-long Petit Bois Island, its French name meaning "little wood." Once a western fragment of Mobile Bay's Dauphin Island, it was separated by a fierce hurricane in 1717. A little farther west, just three miles south of Pascagoula and within sight of land, is pie-shaped Round Island. A 139-year-old lighthouse there was toppled by Hurricane Georges in 1998. Farther out and to the west is the 14-

mile-long wilderness of Horn Island, the crown jewel of the Gulf Islands National Seashore, which was created on January 8, 1971. A safe haven in years gone by for schooners hauling cargoes of shrimp and oysters, the island was occupied from 1845 to 1920 by the Waters family, which farmed and raised livestock there. The U.S. Army used the island to set up an experiment station for chemical and biological warfare, and trained military scout dogs there during World War II. According to Hobbs, the late artist Walter Anderson was captivated by the "fragile windblown solitude" of the island, where he recorded his "observations in water color and other media" during his lifetime. The westernmost island in the chain is T-shaped Cat Island. Lying south of the city of Long Beach, Cat was inhabited from the 1700s for many years by settlers who raised livestock and vegetables for the marketplaces of New Orleans.

Between Horn Island on the east and Cat Island on the west, directly south of Biloxi, lies Ship Island, whose "deep water harbor to the north of the island's lee made it a safe harbor for pirates and other voyagers throughout the centuries, including French explorers." During the War of 1812, the island served as a staging area for 10,000 British soldiers who encamped on its dunes prior to the Battle of New Orleans against Americans commanded by General Andrew Jackson. Fort Massachusetts was constructed on the western tip of the island in 1859—ironically, at the urging of Jefferson Davis, a former U.S. senator, U.S. Secretary of War at the time, and later president of the Confederacy—and Ship Island was occupied by both Confederate and Union troops at one time or another throughout the course of the Civil War. The fort was named in honor of a federal warship that fought in the Mississippi Sound. The island again served as a staging area for federal troops assaulting Mobile Bay and New Orleans, and was used as a holding site for Confederate prisoners in the closing days of the war. Hurricanes over time divided the island into East Ship and West Ship. Hobbs wrote: "The island treasures of the Mississippi Gulf Coast served to provide safe havens and homes to early settlers. The islands also sheltered coast communities from invasion by both natural and human forces."

On February 10, 1699, a small French flotilla under the command of 37-year-old French-Canadian Pierre Le Moyne, Sieur d'Iberville, landed in Mississippi Gulf Coast waters. Iberville, born in New France, Canada, in 1661, fought for France against England in the colonial wars and was assigned to the Gulf of Mexico by the French king, Louis XIV, in 1697. Seeking to find the mouth of the Mississippi River, Iberville set up his base of operations on Ship Island two years later. Exploring the Mississippi coastline, he set out on February 13, 1699, to investigate a column of smoke rising from what probably was Deer Island and made his first contact with local Indians. Once reaching shore on the Biloxi peninsula, he pursued a small party of the local Native Americans, later recording the experience in his journals (historian

Richebourg Gaillard McWilliams is the editor of *Iberville's Gulf Journals*):

> *I crossed over to the land four leagues north of here in my Biscayan with 11 men, and my brother in a bark canoe with two men. I went ashore and there found two trails of Indians made yesterday, which I followed overland with one man, my brother coming alone in the bark canoe and the Biscayan following a half a league behind us to avoid frightening the Indians . . . The approach to the shore is quite shallow: half a league offshore, four feet of water . . . We are seeing many plum trees in bloom; tracks of turkeys, partridges, which are no bigger than quail; hares like the ones in France; some rather good oysters.*

Iberville and his men continued to follow the Indians by canoe the next day and caught up with them onshore, whereupon the Indians fled into the woods, leaving behind one old man who was too sick to run. The Frenchmen conversed with him by hand signals, and gave him food and tobacco. Later, they met up with other Native Americans. "Three of those Indians and two women, having been met by one of my Canadians, came along to sing the calumet of peace to me . . . ," wrote Iberville. "They made a sagamite of Indian corn to feast us. I . . . gave them axes, knives, shirts, tobacco, pipes, tinder boxes and glass beads."

Iberville, utilizing the earlier journals of French explorer René-Robert Cavelier, Sieur de La Salle, subsequently discovered the mouth of the Mississippi River by navigating through the Gulf, erected Fort Maurepas on the eastern side of Biloxi Bay (at the site of present-day Ocean Springs) and sailed for France on May 3, 1699. He died of yellow fever at Havana, Cuba, in 1706, leaving behind the journals of his Gulf Coast exploration. McWilliams noted the rich mixture of French, Spanish, and English adventurers and pioneers who explored and settled the area in pursuit of empire, and "quickly infused the Mississippi Valley and the Gulf Coast with their own cultures, an influence that lasted long after formal English control came to North America."

Historian Val Husley wrote in his book *Biloxi: 300 Years* that, according to French records, there was a "handful of settlers and slaves at Biloxi" between 1723 and 1729. The British gained control of the area in 1763, then relinquished it to Spanish forces in 1781 under the Treaty of Paris, which ended the American Revolution. In 1798, the United States acquired the territory of West Florida, which included the Mississippi Gulf Coast, and opened it up for immigration. The Gulf Coast returned to French possession in 1800, but the U.S. purchase of Louisiana from France in 1803 included West Florida, and the United States "annexed the region between the Pearl and Perdido Rivers to the Mississippi Territory" in 1812. The descendants of the French-speaking settlers who inhabited the Coast in the early seventeenth century, according to Rebecca Larche Moreton in "The French Language of the Coast," have "continued the use of the French language, even as the dominant culture changed from French and Catholic to English and protestant."

Throughout the settlement of the region, hurricanes or the possibility of hurricanes posed a continuing threat to Native Americans, explorers, and pioneers alike. Richard Glaczier, in "The History of Gulf Coast Hurricanes," wrote: "Since Europeans first settled on the shores of what was to become the state of Mississippi, hurricanes of varying intensity have destroyed homes, livestock, jobs and even lives." Dauphin Island was split by the hurricane of 1817, known as Andre Penicaut's Storm, as it slammed into Mobile Bay. Another storm struck the area in 1722, and three hurricanes hit between New Orleans and Pensacola, Florida, in 1778, 1779, and 1780. According to Sullivan, "The Great Louisiana Hurricane of August 19, 1812, scattered the blockading British warships at the mouth of the Mississippi and pushed saltwater 75 miles upriver."

Following the War of 1812, America's second war of independence, rural residents from the poorer areas of Georgia and the Carolinas began immigrating to south Mississippi, but the mixture along the Mississippi Coast proved to be one of oil and water. Two of the coastal counties, Hancock and Harrison, maintained close economic and cultural ties to the diverse, urban populations of New Orleans and Mobile, primarily because of their proximity to those two relatively large cities. Consequently, they distanced themselves from the agrarian interests of the Delta planters and other inland landowners who helped push Mississippi to statehood in 1817.

The state borders of Mississippi, Louisiana, and Alabama were clearly delineated by 1819, but the Mississippi Gulf Coast increasingly assumed the look and feel of New Orleans, with its growing cosmopolitan population of about 25,000, to the west, and of Mobile, with about 2,500 residents, to the east. Biloxi was situated about midway between the two major cities. Wealthy businessmen from the urban areas and aristocratic gentry from the plantations began building homes and summer cottages along the Gulf Coast during the 1820s in an effort to trade city and country discomforts for the seafood, beaches, and salty breezes of the Mississippi Sound. Shieldsboro (renamed Bay St. Louis in 1875), Pass Christian, Biloxi, Ocean Springs, and Pascagoula soon became popular retreats as original pioneer families were joined by a rapidly expanding influx of fishermen, boat builders, merchants, hotel keepers, truck farmers, and other newcomers.

The Compte Delisle, a mapmaker charged in 1699 with remapping coastal waters, named St. Louis Bay for the king of France, and Shieldsboro sprang up on its shore. The town was named in honor of the British general Thomas Shields, who took control and settled the area in 1790. Shieldsboro and the villages immediately to its west—Waveland, Clermont Harbor, and Lakeshore—were popular holiday destinations for New Orleanians and became a melting pot for many different cultures. Visitors to Bay St. Louis found Main Street lined with a large assortment of intact nineteenth century structures as they shopped for art, crafts, and antiques or dined at one of the town's superb eating establishments.

Waveland, considered by many in earlier times to be a suburb of New Orleans, was called Grand Bend and was actually a part of old Shieldsboro until it was granted a separate charter on March 6, 1888. Waveland's Old Pirate House, built in 1802, was, according to legend, owned by Jean Lafitte and had a secret tunnel leading from the house to the waterfront. (The house was destroyed by Camille.) It would be 1928 before a two-mile wooden bridge replaced a ferry boat service to connect Bay St. Louis and Waveland to Henderson Point and Pass Christian, located eastward just across the bay.

New Jersey lawyer John Henderson, who later became a U.S. senator and general of the Mississippi Militia, established his home in 1839 on the westernmost tip of the Pass Christian peninsula that now bears his name. Henderson Point, less than two square miles in size, was dubbed "unannexable" by local residents who steadfastly resisted annexation by Pass Christian.

Pass Christian was explored by Iberville in 1699 during his search for the mouth of the Mississippi River. The city and its small port developed into a trading center during the 1800s, as well as a summer retreat for cotton and cane planters from Mississippi, Alabama, and Louisiana. Located just offshore and extending about two and a half miles in length was one of the best oyster reefs in the world. The reefs were so productive that hundreds of workers, primarily of Yugoslavian and Polish descent, were brought in from Baltimore, Maryland, to work in seafood factories that drove the local economy.

Wealthy New Orleanians built stately mansions and vacation cottages and considered the coast their "playground." The Pass Christian Hotel, built in 1831, closed its doors in 1848 with a social reception for General Zachary Taylor, hero of the Mexican War. As Dan Ellis put it in "Bay St. Louis, Waveland, and Diamondhead": "It was a way of life that thrived on luxury, peacefulness and graciousness." But violence always lurked just around the corner, and, over the course of nearly two centuries, *affaires d' honneur* often were settled under the "dueling oaks," which stand today on the grounds of Pass Christian High School. It was there that New Orleans business rivals E. W. Estlie and Michael Cuddy dueled with pistols on May 21, 1856. Cuddy, a 42-year-old native of Kilkenny, Ireland, was killed. According to Ellis, a marble monument in Pass Christian's Live Oak Cemetery commemorates that "last duel fought in Pass Christian, which ended in vanquishing a man's heart, soul and body."

The town of Long Beach, just east of Pass Christian, originally was designated "Bear Point" on a 1774 British map and was settled by the French family of Nicholas L'Adner. It was also called the Chimneys, Rosalie, and Scott's Station at various times in its history. According to Mary Ellen Alexander in "Long Beach, Mississippi," the city was named Long Beach in 1882 to mark "the long sloping beaches of glistening white sand that lay along its shoreline . . ." Paddle-wheel steamboats operating between New Orleans and Mobile starting in 1827 played a key role in the town's early development, and truck farming later provided a steady boost to the local economy. Many Italians immigrated to Long Beach through the port of New Orleans around the turn of the century, and one section of town, near Seale Avenue and Pineville Road, became known as "Little Italy."

Eastward down the beach, Gulfport developed into a city following the construction of a deep-water port there in 1898. It became the Gulf of Mexico terminus for the Gulf and Ship Island Railroad, built by the former Confederate captain William Harris Hardy, which stretched 70 miles northward through Mississippi's Piney Woods to Hattiesburg, where Hardy was one of the founding fathers. Gulfport's rapid development was initially closely tied to the Mississippi lumber industry and later to the importing of bananas. "The state's vast timber resources gave the port a commodity most European markets desired," Steve Dickerson and Jim Miller wrote in "City of Gulfport."

Mississippi City, a little farther east and now virtually lost in the urban sprawl that connects Gulfport with Biloxi, was created by the 1837 legislature as the county seat of Harrison County because of its central location between Pass Christian and Biloxi. It also was the site of a famous bare-knuckle fight between John L. Sullivan and Paddy Ryan on February 7, 1882, on the lawn of the Barnes Hotel. A historical marker eventually was placed at the U.S. Highway 90 site, one block west of Courthouse Road between Texas and Arkansas streets, to mark the spot where Sullivan was established as the unquestioned world heavyweight champion.

After Iberville established the French beachhead in April 1699 on the eastern shore of Biloxi Bay, site of the city of Ocean Springs, he constructed Fort Maurepas on the peninsula. "The original settlement at Ocean Springs became known as Vieux Biloxy or Old Biloxi," Ray Bellande wrote in "A History of Ocean Springs, Mississippi." A little farther east is Gautier and then Pascagoula, which in earlier history were known as West Pascagoula and East Pascagoula, respectively.

Harrison County, extending from St. Louis Bay eastward to Biloxi Bay, was officially created in 1841 and named in honor of the newly elected president, William Henry Harrison. An early coastal pathway linking Pass Christian with Point Cadet in Biloxi developed into what is known today as Pass Road. The Gulf Coast gained a couple of major landmarks during this antebellum era that have withstood the test of time: the Biloxi Lighthouse, built in 1848, and Beauvoir, completed by wealthy original owner Sarah Dorsey in 1852, which became the final home of the Confederate president, Jefferson Davis, in 1877. It was at Beauvoir, French for "beautiful view," that Davis wrote his memoirs, *The Rise and Fall of the Confederate Government*, published in 1881. The Biloxi Lighthouse was built by the U.S. Lighthouse Service on the western edge of the city. "Perhaps the city's most enduring symbol, the Biloxi Lighthouse guided the area through a period of tremendous growth," wrote Husley.

Transportation—spurred by the proliferation of steamboats and railroads—improved rapidly along the Mississippi Gulf Coast during the decades preceding the 1861 outbreak of war between the states. The dredging of Mobile Bay to the east greatly improved access to the area for seagoing vessels, and construction of a five-mile-long railway from downtown New Orleans to the shores of Lake Ponchartrain allowed residents of the city to board steamboats that traversed the more shallow waters of the Mississippi Sound from port to port. The Great Barbados Hurricane of 1831 destroyed a new pier and terminal at Port Ponchartrain, but the storm represented only a temporary setback to the tourist boom that was enveloping the Coast.

The era of the steamboat flourished along the Coast during the hurricane-free 1840s, with boats docking frequently at Bay St. Louis, Pass Christian, Mississippi City, Biloxi, Ocean Springs, and Pascagoula—affectionately nicknamed the "Six Sisters." Long piers were built far into the shallow waters of the Sound by municipalities, hotels, and beachfront residents to provide easy access to boat travel and recreational pursuits, and Sullivan noted that the "simultaneous application of steam to lumber mills spawned commercial-industrial villages at bay heads and river mouths."

Easy access to the coastal retreats—coupled with a yellow fever epidemic that struck New Orleans in 1853—provided incentive for many of the 150,000 New Orleanians and nearly 30,000 Mobile residents to exchange, as

Sullivan put it, "the stinking sewers, heat, dust and yellow fever of the cities for the Gulf breezes." Biloxi, formerly the smallest of the Mississippi coastal cities, became the largest because of its location midway between Mobile and New Orleans.

The coast was struck again by a major hurricane on August 25, 1852, leaving Pass Road "strewn with pine trees felled by the storm." By 1860, Biloxi's population had reached nearly 900, with foreign-born residents—mostly German, Irish, and French—making up about 28 percent of the inhabitants. The city also included residents from Spain, Italy, England, Scotland, Austria, Denmark, Belgium, Sweden, Mexico, Russia, Canada, and Norway. Twenty-five percent of the city's population came from 23 other states, mostly Louisiana and Alabama, and the rest were native Mississippians. The population of Harrison County had reached about 5,000 residents, not including another 1,000 slaves.

War was fast approaching but, in the meantime, Mother Nature delivered her own dose of trouble to the Mississippi Gulf Coast. Three hurricanes raked the area in the late summer of 1860, destroying the Biloxi waterfront and damaging the Biloxi Lighthouse. Sullivan wrote: "The people of the Mississippi coast, emerging from the devastation of three hurricanes in seven weeks, found themselves embroiled in a political maelstrom of far greater consequence—the winds of war swept the land." The Mississippi Gulf Coast had become a "no-man's land between Yankee-held New Orleans and Confederate Mobile." Mississippi became the second southern state to leave the Union on January 9, 1861, and Coast residents organized the Biloxi Rifles, which subsequently became Company E, Third Mississippi Infantry, in the Confederate Army of the Tennessee. The Coast unit fought in many battles and campaigns, taking heavy casualties late in the war when the one-armed, one-legged Rebel general John Bell Hood dashed his army to pieces in a tactically ill-founded charge across a two-mile-wide field at the Battle of Franklin, Tennessee, just south of Nashville. Unfortunately, a pizza restaurant today marks the high-water mark of that bloody charge on a largely unpreserved battlefield.

The Mississippi Coast economy languished in the aftermath of the war, but steamboat service had resumed by 1865 and the timber industry was recovering from the national ordeal. As Husley noted, "By 1870, track had been laid and there was regular freight and passenger service between New Orleans and Mobile." That provided a big boost to the Biloxi seafood industry. Jefferson Davis, after spending time in a federal prison, moved into Beauvoir with his wife, Varina, in 1877 and began writing his memoirs at the scenic southern home with the "beautiful view" of the Sound. Six hurricanes had struck the Mississippi Coast during the eight years from 1852 to 1860, but "as if ashamed of such excess, Mother Nature pulled her punches for the next 33 years." As the threat of death by wind and water subsided, however, the devil mosquito moved in to take a deadly toll of its own. Murella Hebert

Powell, in "Biloxi, Queen City of the Gulf Coast," wrote, "Yellow fever struck Biloxi in epidemic proportions in the summer of 1878, with 600 cases reported and 45 deaths." This led the National Board of Health to establish a U.S. quarantine station on Ship Island in 1880.

As the market demand for oysters increased, five Biloxi entrepreneurs formed a partnership to construct Biloxi's first seafood cannery. F. William Elmer, William F. Gorenflow, John Maycock, Lazaro Lopez, and William K. M. Ducate organized the Lopez, Elmer & Company in 1881, igniting a seafood boom. Seafood factories sprang up along the coast, and the sails of schooners, carrying cargoes of oysters and other delicacies of the deep, dotted the horizon of the Mississippi Sound in constant procession. Truck farming spurred the growth of Long Beach, as the Coast became an exporter of vegetables, fruit, and pecans. The success of the railroad, combined with technological advances in canning and the production of artificial ice, helped Biloxi, which had 5,000 residents, vie with Baltimore, Maryland, to be known as the "Seafood Capital of the world."

The prosperity of the late 1800s, however, was about to be interrupted by the first major storm in more than three decades, as Mother Nature's punching power was restored. A powerful storm slammed into the Gulf Coast in 1893, killing approximately 2,000 between Grand Isle, Louisiana, and Pascagoula, and smashing the Biloxi fishing fleet on Lake Borgne and in the Louisiana marshes. All waterfront communities were heavily damaged, all but three of 100 vessels sheltered behind Deer Island were sunk, the canneries on Biloxi's Point Cadet were destroyed, and a large section of the Biloxi Bay railroad bridge was knocked out. "The cat-and-mouse game ended with the October hurricane of 1893—not the strongest in Mississippi-Louisiana history, just the most murderous," wrote Sullivan. Most of the victims died in an area north of Grand Isle, Louisiana, as winds reached 130 miles per hour. An estimated 1,650 men, women, and children drowned in the town of Cheniere Caminada, where all but six structures were leveled and only 150 inhabitants survived. Only about 100 died in Mississippi, but the damage in both states exceeded $1 million. South Louisiana experienced a storm surge of about 15 feet, while the surge along the Mississippi Coast reached 9.3 feet. The barometric pressure reached a low recording of 28.65. Wrote Sullivan: "Biloxi boasted five major seafood canneries by 1893, and they all fell victim to the October storm."

Gulf Coast residents had been thoroughly shocked by the first major storm in 33 years. Although the U.S. Weather Service had been in existence for 23 years prior to the October storm of 1893, Coast residents had received no early warnings. The hurricane advertised the area's alarming vulnerability to destruction from the sea, the need for stricter building codes, and the necessity of better predisaster and postdisaster planning by local, state, and federal agencies. "But the dawning recognition of these facts lagged far behind the implementation of programs designed to protect a growing population that lived on an increasingly built-up coastline at the mercy of future hurricanes," Sullivan asserted.

Increasingly, trains were replacing steamboats as the primary mode of transporting people and goods to and from the Mississippi Coast in the late nineteenth century. Completion of the Gulf and Ship Island Railroad between Gulfport and Hattiesburg in September of 1896 marked the first time the coast "was directly connected to the cities of the north." Biloxi entered the twentieth century as the Coast's largest city, with a population approaching 7,000. Although no hurricane struck the Mississippi Coast in 1900, one did strike Galveston, Texas, that year, killing 6,000 in one of the most devastating storms in U.S. history. In Biloxi, it was a fire that wreaked havoc. Shortly after midnight on November 9, 1900, a devastating fire erupted in the rear of Kennedy's saloon on Reynoir Street. The flames, driven by shifting winds, roared down Reynoir and Fayard streets, east and west through the business district, and down the beach, destroying ninety structures.

Another hurricane, with winds ranging from 80 to 90 miles an hour, struck a glancing blow on the Mississippi Coast in 1901 and deepened "the new deep-water channel being dredged from the harbor at Ship Island to the mainland at Gulfport." Hurricanes in 1906 and 1909 also "caused considerable destruction to property and some loss of life." The 1906 hurricane (in September) "set a new record for size and longevity," claiming about 100 lives and causing an estimated $11 million in damage along the storm's inland track to Hattiesburg. The 1909 hurricane punished Louisiana more than it did Mississippi. It took about 350 lives and caused about $3 million in damages in the Pelican State, while killing nine persons and causing about $2 million worth of damage on the Mississippi Coast.

After a six-year respite, on September 29, 1915, a hurricane of awesome proportions aimed its unprecedented fury at the Louisiana and Mississippi coasts. The West Indian storm had sustained wind speeds of 140 miles per hour, the highest in North American history at the time, and "a barometric reading of 28.11 inches, the record low in American weather" when it came ashore at Grand Isle, Louisiana, at 6:50 p.m. In Mississippi, the hurricane destroyed the Biloxi Yacht Club, leveled large stands of timber on the Coast and beyond, disrupted a three-day reunion of Confederate veterans, scattered oak trees across the lawn at Beauvoir, and demolished an amusement park that had just opened for business the year before on nearby Deer Island. Trolley tracks west of the lighthouse were undermined and bent out of shape, and oyster schooners and other watercraft lay beached all along the shore. Many lives and vessels were lost as seventy Biloxi schooners were caught in the open waters of the Louisiana marshes. Despite the considerable damage around Biloxi, most of the 18 deaths in Mississippi occurred from Gulfport west. "Minus 200 feet of her seawall, half of her downtown area and most of her beach road along with huge chunks of bluff, Bay St. Louis had suffered terribly," Sullivan noted.

Less than a year later, on July 5, 1916, another hurricane, packing winds of 80 to 100 miles an hour, blasted the Mississippi Coast for 16 hours, knocking down Biloxi's hanging street lamps and toppling the statue of a Confederate soldier "off his marble pedestal at the Harrison County Courthouse" in Gulfport. "For the sixth time in 23 years, the people of the Mississippi Coast cleaned up after a Gulf cyclone." And, according to Powell, "Again, concerned citizens pressed for seashore protection, but action was delayed by America's entrance into World War I." During those years before America's entry into the war, wrote Husley, "Biloxi continued to modernize. New businesses appeared, banking expanded and parcel post service arrived." It would be more than three decades before a major hurricane would again visit the Mississippi Gulf Coast.

Although World War I delayed construction plans for a badly needed seawall along the Mississippi Coast, the economic prosperity that accompanied the Roaring '20s following the war brought a renewed effort to get the job done. Harrison County residents approved a $2 million bond issue to build a 24-mile-long concrete seawall from Biloxi to Pass Christian, and construction got under way in 1924 on "reportedly the longest structure of its kind in the world." The project was completed in 1927 and dedicated on May 1, 1928, dramatically changing "the ambiance of the Biloxi waterfront." Sullivan noted that neighboring coastal counties soon followed suit as "Hancock County walled 14 miles of the west side of the Bay of

St. Louis and Jackson County built two, two-mile walls to protect Ocean Springs and Pascagoula beachfronts."

The 1920s also marked the emergence of the automobile age, and hotels such as the Buena Vista, Avelez, and Tivoli opened their doors in Biloxi. Wrote Husley: "Biloxi's 10,937 residents witnessed the replacement of horses and wagons and the electric streetcar by automobiles and a modern bus system." The new seawall also provided protection for construction of a new beachfront highway, the first transcoastal highway, later known as U.S. 90. A part of the Old Spanish Trail national highway route from St. Augustine, Florida, to San Diego, California, it covered the Mississippi Coast from the Alabama line to the Pearl River.

"By 1930, automobile bridges spanned every river and bay between New Orleans and Mobile, resulting in the first ferryless ride between the two cities," wrote Sullivan. Before the seawall was completed, however, it was tested on September 21, 1926, by the remnants of a hurricane that killed about 300 people and caused $100 million in property damage in Florida, but did little more than knock out utility lines in Mississippi.

The Prohibition Era that accompanied the Roaring '20s produced a curious resort project on the shifting sands of Dog Keys—two islands that lay 13 miles southeast of Biloxi between Ship and Horn islands. The larger of the Dog Keys, Dog Island, was three miles long and more than a quarter-mile wide, resting on a shallow stretch of shoals. It was there that Colonel J. W. Apperson, owner of the Buena Vista Hotel, Walter "Skeet" Hunt, and Arbeau Caillavet created the Isle of Caprice Amusement Company and, according to Husley, "constructed a resort—complete with liquor and gambling—outside of U.S. jurisdiction . . ." Promoted as the Isle of Caprice, it opened for business in 1926, with three schooners providing transportation to and from the island. However, a few years later, Powell wrote, the "shifting sand key, technically not an island at all and having no foundation . . . shifted." Husley described it this way: "The Isle of Caprice's main pavilion offered casino gambling and contained a restaurant which reportedly served almost 1,000 guests nightly. The venture lasted until 1931 when the methodical loss of the island's grasses and trees caused it to be reclaimed by the Sound. For decades thereafter, the island's location was marked by a pipe spewing cool artesian water into the Gulf." Hunt eventually became sole owner of the "island," and his heirs continue to pay taxes on it.

No hurricanes struck the Mississippi Coast during the 1930s and, although it was the era of the Great Depression throughout America, the Coast continued to make steady progress on a variety of fronts. The Biloxi airport project, on property that included the Biloxi Golf Club, Naval Reserve Park, and Biloxi Stadium, was launched in 1929 and continued throughout the 1930s. In 1941, the site would be included in the construction of Keesler Field, which became Keesler Air Force Base in 1947. It was named in honor of Lieutenant Samuel Reeves Keesler, Jr., an aerial observer killed in Europe during World War I and the son of a retired major general who was mayor of the city of Greenwood, Mississippi, at the time. A new two-lane bridge on U.S. 90 opened across the mouth of Biloxi Bay in 1933 and the Biloxi Veterans Affairs medical facility, which opened in August of that year, "was heralded by city leaders as the greatest accomplishment in city history." In 1938, Ingalls Shipbuilding began its massive and nationally important operations at Pascagoula. But there was more yet to come. In 1941, according to Husley, "Biloxi offered the Air Corps 832 acres of land [the Keesler Field site] as a site for an air technical school." Three weeks after the surprise Japanese attack on the U.S. fleet at Pearl Harbor, which occurred on December 7, 1941, and brought America into World War II, Gulfport secured a naval construction battalion (or "Seabee") base. The U.S. Merchant Marine Cadet Training School opened on Henderson Point on September 15, 1942, and Ingalls sent nearly 100 vessels on their way to the Allies as the war heated up. Sullivan wrote: "The wisteria-like growth of restaurants, motels, and other businesses catering to tourists who came via the highway [U.S. 90] resulted in a blaze of neon, igniting long strips from Pascagoula to Bay St. Louis. The 1947 coast presented an enticing and closely packed target for the Storm King."

Indeed, the "Storm King" did not fail to find the "enticing" target. The first major hurricane in 31 years struck the Florida, Mississippi, and Louisiana coasts on September 19, 1947. With a 25-mile-wide eye and a barometric pressure of 28.61, the storm hit Florida first, picked up strength again over the Gulf, then slammed into the Mississippi Gulf Coast and New Orleans. With winds of 150 miles per hour, the powerful right front quadrant forced a 15-foot wall of water across the untested seawall and undermined the highway beyond. The water surged for more than a block into Biloxi, leaving only the Biloxi Yacht Club and the USO building standing south of U.S. 90. Surprisingly, only one person was killed in Biloxi, but more than $17.5 million in damage was reported. "The seafood industry on Biloxi's Point Cadet was devastated and tourism along the waterfront . . . was crippled," Husley noted.

In terms of loss of life, other parts of the Mississippi Coast were not as fortunate. All totaled, 20 Mississippians died in the storm, including five deaths each at Clermont Harbor and Waveland and two in Lakeshore, bringing the death toll in Hancock County to 12; eight were dead in Harrison County, including five in Long Beach and one each in Gulfport, Mississippi City, and Biloxi. President Harry Truman "declared Florida, Louisiana and Mississippi—with their whopping total of $110 million in damage—to be disaster areas."

As residents cleared the wreckage of the Coast's first major hurricane since 1916, one thing became immediately clear: the nearly 20-year-old seawall on which so much trust had been placed did not prevent extensive damage all along the beaches of Harrison and Hancock counties. It had been breached in several places. So, local leaders would act swiftly on the Federal Beach Erosion Board's 1944 recommendation that a sand beach was needed to buffer the driving force of wind and water, and the U.S. Army Corps of Engineers undertook the project in 1951. The "longest man-made beach in the world" (24 miles long and 300 feet wide) was completed in 1954 and, with the federal government's widening of U.S. 90 into four lanes, became one of the Mississippi Gulf Coast's and Biloxi's most popular tourist attractions.

In addition, a second seawall was built about 250 feet south of the old wall, and some backfilling along the beach side of the highway created even more useable acreage. Wrote Husley: "The combination of sand beach and superhighway led to the development of the 'West Beach strip,' a 6,000-foot-long recreational business district just beyond Biloxi's western city limits." New building codes were implemented by Harrison County and each of its municipalities. The codes restricted advertising signs and beachfront construction but provided exemptions for structures already in place. With the aid of a federal grant, officials also created the Harrison County Civil Defense Council.

Julia Guice would become volunteer director of plans and training for Biloxi civil defense operations in 1957. "With those moves, preparations for, monitoring and response to storms and other disasters took on a county-wide coordinated effort," wrote Glaczier. After the National Weather Service began giving feminine names to hurricanes in 1953, the Mississippi Coast would be visited by weak Hurricane Flossy in 1956 and in 1960 by Hurricane Ethel, which packed 150-mile-an-hour winds but collided with a cold front and fell apart between Biloxi and Pascagoula.

The seafood industry on the Mississippi Coast was a bit slow in reacting to the increased consumer demand that followed World War II, but gained momentum in 1950 when exploratory fishing by the U.S. Fish and Wildlife Service confirmed shrimping grounds east and west of the Delta area around the mouth of the Mississippi River. Local oyster production also quadrupled during the 1960s following the regulation of oyster harvesting. Biloxi became the state's second-largest city, ranking in size only behind the state capital of Jackson.

The 1960s also marked a turbulent era in Mississippi and other parts of the nation on the civil rights front, and the Gulf Coast was not untouched by the winds of change. Confrontations between blacks and whites near the Biloxi Lighthouse in 1959 and 1960, according to Powell, "sparked the eventual complete integration of Mississippi Coast beaches." The 24-mile-long, man-made beach in Harrison County—stretching from St. Louis Bay on the western end to Biloxi Bay in the east—is about 100–150 yards wide, running along the south side of U.S. Highway 90. Fronting the beach on the north side of the highway is a string of large homes and antebellum mansions, interspersed with hotels, motels, restaurants, harbors, shopping centers, and other businesses. African-Americans who ventured onto the beach during the Jim

Crow era, however, faced the likelihood of harassment by white ruffians, nearby property owners, and/or law enforcement officers. Nevertheless, a brave group of blacks began using a portion of the beach in front of the Veterans Administration Hospital in Gulfport, setting the stage for more demonstrations that followed.

On Thursday, May 14, 1959, nine black citizens of Biloxi consciously defied white segregationists by visiting another popular site on the beach favored by locals. They were removed by police and warned not to return, but as local physician and civil rights activist Gilbert Mason recalled, according to James Patterson Smith, "Additional wade-ins at Biloxi the following April [1960] triggered the bloodiest race riot in Mississippi history and produced the first significant U.S. Justice Department intervention in Mississippi to challenge the state's segregation laws in federal court." In a front-page story on April 30, 1960, that is cited in Mason's book, *Beaches, Blood, and Ballots: A Black Doctor's Civil Rights Struggle*, James L. Hicks of the *Amsterdam News* called the Biloxi wade-ins "the beginning of the civil rights movement in Mississippi."

Hurricane Betsy swept the Mississippi Gulf Coast on September 9, 1965, after striking Louisiana with winds gusting to 100 miles an hour and tides ranging from 10 to 15 feet. The newly appointed civil defense team of Wade and Julia Guice guided the Coast population's storm preparedness with the aid of new satellite photography and information from hurricane-seeking aircraft. Biloxi's commercial buildings, central beach area, and western strip, as in 1947, received heavy damage. The heavier toll, however, came in neighboring Louisiana where dozens of lives were lost and thousands were made homeless. Husley wrote: "In Betsy's wake, Harrison County supervisors enacted measures to prevent illegal structures from being built along the beach." The wisdom of their efforts bore fruit four years later.

President Lyndon Johnson flew into New Orleans to survey Louisiana losses, estimated at $1 billion. Mississippi's governor, Paul B. Johnson, Jr., appraised his state's damage at $10 million. The only Mississippi Coast resident who had anything positive to say about Betsy was Wade Guice. "Hurricane Betsy was an excellent training device," he said. "She pointed out some deficiencies that we had in particular with an integrated [storm preparedness] system. And we were able to patch an awful lot of those holes."

Lessons learned from Betsy were to pay off just four years later when the Mississippi Coast, as Sullivan put it, "took a direct hit from a storm that made Betsy look like a third-grade fistfight on the playground."

HUNRÁKEN

The Mayan storm god, Hunraken, haunted the Caribbean coasts of tropical Mexico many centuries ago, indiscriminately meting out death and destruction to the helpless Indians who had the misfortune to cross his path and instilling fear and apprehension in the hearts and minds of those who survived his terrifying grasp. The evil spirit, or mythological personification of the "big wind" depicted in Mayan hieroglyphics, may be the "first human record of Atlantic tropical cyclones," according to Edward Rappaport and Jose Fernandez in their article "The Deadliest Atlantic Tropical Cyclones, 1492–Present." Other ancient Indian civilizations knew him by similar names—Hyuracan, Hurakan, Huracan, and Aracan. Mysterious and unpredictable quirks of nature, hurricanes have been around since the beginning of time. They have scourged successive cultures for thousands of years, long before weather records came into existence, randomly assaulting human beings' fragile works and peace of mind. They are, without a doubt, nature's most destructive combination of heat, wind, and water. They are the most powerful storms on earth.

According to geologists, layers of sediment at the bottom of a lake in Alabama appear to have been deposited there by hurricane storm surges from the nearby Gulf of Mexico some three thousand years ago. Sediment cores from the west coast of Florida also provide evidence of extensive freshwater floods caused by hurricanes a thousand years ago. The ancient Indian inhabitants of the Mississippi Gulf Coast—the Biloxis, Pascagoulas, and Acolapissas—most certainly experienced the wrath of Hunraken, although they left no written record. Based on current Atlantic tropical cyclone activity, estimates are that as many as 5,000 storm systems likely developed during the past five centuries, some dying away without causing harm and others creating death tolls that were never documented.

It was only with the European conquest of North America that documentation of hurricane events became a part of recorded history. Columbus wrote about his encounter with an Atlantic hurricane during his fourth voyage to the New World. Spanish explorers subsequently adopted the Indian word for the big wind, *huracán*, into their language and that evolved into hurricane. The royal fleet of the Spanish conquistador Cabeza de Vaca was wrecked by a hurricane off the coast of Cuba in 1527, delaying his plans to occupy a portion of Florida. In 1559, a great storm battered the fleet of Spanish explorer Tristan de Luna as he was attempting to establish a settlement at Ochusa, or present-day Pensacola, Florida. Some historians believe a hurricane was responsible for the strange disappearance of the "Lost Colony" settlement on Roanoke Island in 1588. When a hurricane struck a fleet of ships carrying settlers from England to Virginia in 1609, some of the ships were grounded at Bermuda. The stranded passengers became the first inhabitants of that island nation and their tales of adventure later inspired Shakespeare's writing of *The Tempest*. Among stranded passengers from the sinking vessel, *Sea Venture*, was John Rolfe, future husband of Pocahontas.

The growth of Atlantic coastal populations during the eighteenth century created a greater vulnerability to tropical storms, both on land and at sea, which continued throughout the century. Rappaport and Fernandez wrote: "These shipborne explorers, emigrants, combatants, fishermen, traders, pirates, privateers, slaves and tourists made up the crews and passengers of an uncounted, but enormous number of local transatlantic sailings. Most of the ships traveled to or from the ports of Spain, France, Great Britain and the Netherlands. They usually proved no match for the intense inner-core region of a severe tropical cyclone."

A fierce hurricane blasted New Orleans in 1722, causing the Mississippi River to rise eight feet and leaving devastation from the inland Mississippi River town of Natchez, Mississippi, to Mobile, Alabama, on the Gulf. The storm destroyed more than 35 houses, a church, and a hospital in New Orleans, and wrecked all ships in port there. In 1722, teenager Alexander Hamilton, then living in the West Indies, wrote about the impact of a hurricane there for a local newspaper. "His writing caught the attention of the local gentry, who then raised money to send him to the mainland colonies to further his education, thus setting the stage for his political career," wrote Roger A. Pielke, Jr., and Roger A. Pielke, Sr., in *Hurricanes: Their Nature and Impacts on Society*. A major storm swept over West Florida in 1779 and once again zeroed in on New Orleans, blowing down houses and heavily damaging the fleet of the Spanish governor, Bernado de Gálvez, who was then planning an attack on the British. Although his plans were delayed, Gálvez later accomplished his mission of driving the British out of the Mississippi area. Though Hunraken would continue his cyclical pattern in varying scales of violence throughout the nineteenth and twentieth centuries, the great hurricane of 1780, which killed approximately 22,000 persons in the Lesser Antilles, remains today the ultimate killer storm.

Ship losses related to Atlantic tropical storms continued well into the early 1900s, until technological advances in meteorology, communication, navigation, and marine construction began to mitigate the frequency of such disasters at sea. During the twentieth century, on average, two major hurricanes hit the U.S. coastline somewhere every three years. Between 1900 and 1982, 136 hurricanes affected the U.S. coast, including 55 major storms. The fact that 71,000 deaths were attributed to hurricanes during the 1900s—despite improved forecasting, communications, and warning systems—appears to be linked to increased populations along storm-prone coastal areas. It is interesting to note that five of the deadliest tropical cyclones (the great hurricane of 1780, the Galveston hurricane of 1900, the Dominican Republic storm of 1930, Flora in Haiti and Cuba in 1963, and Fifi in Honduras in 1974) account for about one-third of all hurricane deaths over the past 500 years. "In fact, the ten deadliest storms, while representing . . . less than 0.2 percent of all tropical cyclones since 1492, account for almost one-half of the [200,000] deaths," wrote Rappaport and Fernandez. Most of the deaths were caused by drowning, rather than by wind or other factors.

The terrible Galveston hurricane of 1900 is remembered today as the deadliest natural disaster in U.S. history, killing more Americans than the Chicago fire, San Francisco earthquake, and Johnstown flood all put together. The Category 4 storm slammed into the island city on the morning of September 8, 1900, completely destroying the once-prosperous Texas seaport and leaving at least 6,000 dead in its wake. The storm surge swept over the island and demolished the only bridge to the mainland, trapping the city's 20,000 residents and leveling most structures. The exact death toll will never be known because many of the bodies were not recovered, and the pleasant Gulf breezes had attracted an undetermined number of strangers who had been living temporarily near the beach. The twentieth century had opened, literally, with a bang—and more was in store.

The Mobile-Pensacola hurricane of September 27, 1906, a Category 3 storm packing winds of 120 miles per hour, inundated those two Gulf Coast cities and killed 134 people. On September 20, 1909, the Grand Isle hurricane, a Category 4 storm, killed more than 350 people and "forever changed the landscape of Louisiana" south of New Orleans. Two Category 4 storms struck the Gulf Coast in 1915, one hitting New Orleans and the other again targeting the city of Galveston. The 1915 New Orleans hurricane killed 275 people and "caused Lake Pontchartrain to overflow its banks." The 1915 Galveston hurricane was actually stronger than its 1900 predecessor, but the construction of a seawall and other hurricane defense measures taken since the turn of the century limited the death toll to 275.

The Labor Day hurricane of 1935 was the most powerful storm ever to hit the United States, with sustained winds of 155 m.p.h. and gusts exceeding 200 m.p.h. The full-fledged Category 5 hurricane—one of only three Category 5 storms ever to strike the United States— smashed into the Florida Keys on September 3, leveling Matecumbe Key and destroying the railroad that connected the Keys to the mainland. The official death toll was 423, including 164 civilians and 259 World War I veterans who were residing in three federal rehabilitation camps. "There were so many dead people and no place to take them. They stacked them up and burned them," remembered survivor Jack Russell, who was just 17 at the time of the hurricane. The hurricane had formed rapidly only a few hundred miles off the Florida coast and intensified quickly, leaving little time for evacuation, a "nightmare scenario for hurricane forecasters" today.

The Category 4 Florida-Mississippi hurricane of 1947 (this was before the practice of assigning women's names to hurricanes was initiated) hit the Gulf Coast of Florida on September 17, then banged into Mississippi with Category 3 power two days later, killing 61 people and causing more than $1 billion in damage in modern dollars. Hurricane Hilda took 39 lives and caused half a billion dollars in damage when the Category 3 storm made landfall in Louisiana with winds of 120 m.p.h. in 1964, the second major hurricane that year. The unpredictable Hurricane Betsy appeared to be curving out to sea when it suddenly stalled and turned its Category 3 power on southern Miami and the Florida Keys on September 8, 1965, then roared on to Louisiana on the 10th. The storm claimed 75 lives and caused $6.5 billion in damage by today's financial standards. The Mississippi Gulf Coast residents between Florida and Louisiana didn't know it at the time, but Betsy would be only a tune-up for the fury of the nation's second-ever Category 5 storm, Hurricane Camille, just four years later.

Hurricane Frederic, a powerful Category 3 storm in 1979, was the first major storm to hit the Gulf Coast coastline following Camille a decade earlier. Frederic brought 130 m.p.h. winds and a 15-foot storm surge to the city of Mobile, causing $3.5 billion in damage along the Alabama-Mississippi coastline and making it one of the worst storms in American history. On the other side of the globe that same year, a reconnaissance plane recorded a world-record low atmospheric pressure of 25.69 inches during super Typhoon Tip. Hurricane Gilbert in 1988 was a Category 5 storm—with a record-low Western Hemisphere barometric pressure of 26.13—but it struck Cozumel, Mexico, leaving U.S. shores untouched. This nation's only other Category 5 storm was Hurricane Andrew, the "costliest hurricane in U.S. history." Originally cited as a Category 4 hurricane and upgraded to Category 5 status in 2002, Andrew caused more than $30 billion in damage in south Florida on August 23, 1992. It packed 165 m.p.h. winds, but because 700,000 out of a million people in its path were safely evacuated, the death toll was under fifty. Hurricane Georges left a trail of destruction across the Caribbean region and southern U.S. Gulf Coast September 21–30, 1998, producing wind gusts up to 85 m.p.h., 25-foot waves, heavy flooding, and nearly $6 billion in damage in the United States and Puerto Rico. An estimated 600 persons were reported killed or missing across the islands of the Caribbean, but only four fatalities occurred in the United States.

Hurricanes have been such a consistent factor in the history of Florida that use of the word has been woven into the state's social and cultural fabric. Athletic teams at the University of Miami are called the Hurricanes, as are many little league baseball teams throughout the state. The term is applied to everything from nightclubs to water-park rides. In New Orleans's French Quarter, a favorite watering hole, Pat O'Brien's, features the "Hurricane" as a specialty drink of the house. Ernest Hemingway wrote about them, and there were memorable hurricane scenes in John Huston's film *Key Largo*, starring Humphrey Bogart, Lauren Bacall, and Edward G. Robinson.

Hurricanes have their origin in the heat of the tropics, starting as simple thunderclouds and evolving into massive storms that may live for days or weeks or may die off over cooler waters. Although meteorologists have studied at length the conditions from which hurricanes emerge—falling barometric pressure and rising currents of warm, moist air—they still do not know specifically which factors throw "these delicately balanced and complex conditions out of their normal equilibriums and into the beginnings of a powerful tropical cyclone." Known as typhoons in the western Pacific and as cyclones in the Indian Ocean, they form in all tropical oceans except the South Atlantic and the southeast Pacific. The Philippines, Taiwan, China, and Japan have been hit frequently by Pacific typhoons. Strong easterly winds, however, tend to keep the killer storms away from Hawaii and the West Coast of the United States. Also, the waters of the Gulf Stream along the U.S. East Coast are quite warm (over 80 degrees Fahrenheit) in comparison with West Coast waters, providing greater fuel for Atlantic storms to grow and intensify. Although not predictable on a small-area basis, the storms occur annually within the Atlantic and Gulf states, with an average of two major hurricanes crossing the U.S. coastline in the region every three years since the beginning of the twentieth century. As old as the oceans themselves, "seasonal cyclones and their counterparts around the globe are the greatest storms on earth, killing more people worldwide than all other storms combined."

Although the sun's radiation reaches its peak in June in the tropical Northern Hemisphere, it takes time for the ocean to warm to a great enough depth to support tropical cyclone development. The warmer ocean surface must mix with the cooler water below and that takes more time, usually into the late summer or early fall. Warm ocean temperatures (at least 80 degrees Fahrenheit) must combine with a preexisting disturbance, thunderstorms and high upper-level winds in order for a tropical cyclone to form. Such disturbances typically emerge every three or four days from the coast of Africa as tropical waves. Then, according to the National Oceanic and Atmospheric Administration article "Basics: Origin and Life Cycle," the following occurs:

> Heat and energy for the storm are gathered by the disturbance through contact with warm ocean waters. The winds near the ocean surface spiral into the disturbance's low pressure area. The warm ocean waters add moisture and heat to the air, which rises. As the moisture condenses into drops, more heat is released, contributing additional energy to power the storm. Bands of thunderstorms form and the storm's cloud tops rise higher into the atmosphere. If the winds at these high levels remain relatively light (little or

no wind shear), the storm can remain intact and continue to strengthen.

The early stages of these events may be picked up by satellites as tropical depressions (winds of less than 38 miles per hour), which can begin to take on the familiar spiral appearance with the air of wind flow and the earth's natural rotation. The cyclone becomes a tropical storm when winds reach between 39 to 73 miles per hour and gain hurricane status as the winds reach a minimum of 74 miles per hour. The cloud-free hurricane eye usually forms at this time, as quickly sinking air at the center dries and warms the area.

Hurricane winds whirl in a large spiral around the eye, a relatively calm center that averages about 14 miles wide. Its 100-mile core of thunderclouds and torrential rain has been compared to "a squashed doughnut that spreads out as far as 300 miles from its hole in the middle . . . a pinwheel of Coriolis force bigger than any other weather in its way," as Eric Sloane wrote in *The Book of Storms*. The Coriolis force was named after French mathematician Gaspard-Gustave de Coriolis, who discovered the "turn-to-the-right law." Hurricane winds in the Northern Hemisphere turn in a counterclockwise motion around the eye, while hurricane winds circulate clockwise in the Southern Hemisphere. Sloane described the eye of a hurricane this way:

The strangest experience of any storm is probably to behold the eye of a great hurricane. Just as you are becoming numbed to the fury of wind and rain, an untimely lull will occur. The roar of the storm recedes. The noise of the rain, like continuous thunder, moves away like an echo. The unnatural quiet which takes over makes the hurricane of a moment ago seem a memory. The rain stops now, but an uncertain drizzle continues. A sudden change of temperature dries the air and you have the sensation of stepping into an oven . . . There is no wind . . . You are within a great quiet amphitheater of dark cloud walls. You are at the bottom of the well that is the hub of the hurricane.

The late CBS newsman Edward R. Murrow, after once flying into the eye of a great storm while aboard a hurricane-hunting aircraft, later noted, "If an adequate definition of humility is ever written, it's likely to be done in the eye of a hurricane."

Human beings, with all their scientific know-how, have never been able to alter the strength of a hurricane. Considering that an ordinary summer thunderstorm has energy equivalent to 13 atomic bombs, scientists estimate that the energy of a hurricane in a 24-hour period would equal about 500,000 atomic bombs. Dr. Hal Gerrish, in "Hurricanes: General Background," wrote, "If the energy [of a hurricane] could be converted to electrical energy with only a 3 percent efficiency, the energy in a hurricane in just 24 hours would supply all of the electrical needs of the U.S. for six months."

Hurricane-force winds deliver punishing results to everything in their path, on land and at sea, man-made materials as well as nature's own handiwork. Beasts and fowl are affected, with birds especially suffering tremendously from the impact, some being blown hundreds of miles from their normal habitats. An increase in wind speed adds pressure against objects at a disproportionate rate. The force mounts with the square of the wind speed, meaning that "a three-fold increase in wind speed gives a nine-fold increase in pressure . . . In 75 mph winds, that force becomes 450 pounds; and in 125 mph winds, it becomes 1,250 pounds." During a hurricane gust at Guadeloupe on July 26, 1825, a one-inch-thick wooden plank was driven completely through the trunk of a palm tree 16 inches in diameter. Small wonder that large buildings and lesser structures crumble against such wind velocity. In addition, the winds stir up and carry a barrage of debris and other life-threatening missiles and spawn deadly tornadoes that often create their own toll of human suffering many miles from the eye of the storm. Hurricane Beulah "set a record when it struck the coast of Texas in 1967 and spawned over 150 twisters across the Texas countryside." Also critically influencing the severity of an approaching storm are such other factors as orientation, forward speed, diameter, timing of lunar tides, and geographical features of the region.

Despite the threat posed by wind, a hurricane's most destructive work usually results from the storm surge—a 20-to-30-foot rise in the wind-driven sea, which gains size and momentum as it heads for shore over a gradually shallowing sea floor. The large dome of water, sometimes

50 to 100 miles wide, is topped by an additional layer of battering waves that undermine buildings, gush over seawalls and highways, turn mountains of floating debris into battering rams, and provide watery graves for many unable or unwilling to flee. Combined with the wind, the storm surge sweeps everything in its path, creating even more havoc if it happens to arrive at a time of high tide. Ninety percent of hurricane-related fatalities in the United States are attributed to storm surges. Most of the 6,000 victims of the 1900 Galveston hurricane drowned. Hurricane Camille produced a 24-foot storm surge on top of a 10-foot tide when it hit the Mississippi Gulf Coast in 1969, and Hurricane Hugo brought a 20-foot storm surge to the South Carolina coastline in 1989. Jay Barnes, in *Florida's Hurricane History*, notes, "Under these extreme conditions, it is not difficult to understand why nine out of 10 hurricane-related deaths are attributed to drowning."

Hurricanes usually lose heat energy and begin to decline as they move over cooler water, are torn apart by wind shear, or move inland, where the storm's main moisture source shuts off and surface circulation is reduced by the friction of mountains and other land barriers. The decay rate may depend on the storm's intensity and forward motion at landfall, but they generally weaken to tropical storm status within six to twelve hours and become tropical depressions within about 18 hours. They can reintensify, however, after moving over land areas, such as the Florida peninsula, and renewing their source of energy after exiting the opposite coast. A dying hurricane also may produce heavy rains that can cause major flooding in areas many miles from the storm's coastal landfall, especially in mountainous areas that are more vulnerable to flash floods. A typical hurricane brings six to twelve inches of rainfall to the area it crosses, but some have brought much more. The remnants of Hurricane Agnes in 1972 sparked the disastrous floods along the entire Atlantic tier of states, causing 118 deaths and about $2.1 billion in property damage just from the flooding. Hurricane Floyd in 1999 spawned drenching rains that produced record flooding in North Carolina, where, Barnes wrote in "Jay Barnes on Hurricanes," the "state and local officials were slow to grasp the time-delayed impact of the disaster." The 24-hour rainfall record for the United States was established by Hurricane Easy on the west coast of Florida on September 5–6, 1950, until 1979, when tropical storm Claudette dumped 42 inches of rain on Alvin, Texas.

Despite their power to destroy property and lives, hurricanes nevertheless provide some beneficial functions, such as helping maintain a balance of heat on planet earth. About 80 tropical storms and hurricanes world-wide help transport excess heat from tropical latitudes. "Without them, the tropics would be too hot and the poles too cold," wrote Gerrish. They also provide life-sustaining water in some areas of the world.

As the pressure of wind drops from high to low, the earth's rotation helps produce a whirling movement of air and water that may "divorce itself from the earth contours" and let global law take over. Storm mechanisms create either stirring, pushing, or lifting disturbances, and stirred storms are called cyclonic. Working for British shipping interests in Calcutta in the late 1830s, Captain Henry Piddington, president of the Marine Courts in India, coined the word "cyclone" while studying tropical storms in that region of the world. He noted the peculiar whirling motion of storm clouds and called such weather disturbances cyclones, from the Greek word *kyklon*, meaning coiled or whirling around. The word became a general term for all rotary storms with wind, clouds, and low atmospheric pressure at the center. About sixty tropical waves form each year in the Atlantic, Caribbean, and Gulf of Mexico and, on average, ten reach tropical cyclone or tropical storm intensity. Six may strengthen to hurricane force, and two of those probably will strike the U.S. coastline somewhere between Texas and Maine.

It was not until World War II that military weather forecasters began giving women's names to significant storms. The World Meteorological Organization started listing them alphabetically in 1950 according to the phonetic military radio code, and the first Atlantic hurricane of the season that year was called Able. "Feminists urged the WMO to add men's names, which was done in 1979." Six lists of names are now used on a repeating basis in the Atlantic basin, with an A name picked for the first storm of the season. One list is used one year and another the following year, with each list having 21 names. After the sixth year, the first list is repeated. Dutch, English, French, Spanish, and American names are used on the lists because of the various nationalities affected by Atlantic hurricanes. Women's names are alternated with men's names. "Names of outstanding hurricanes that have been particularly destructive . . . are retired . . . and new names are selected by the World Meteorological Organization as replacements."

Hurricanes are rated 1–5 on the Saffir-Simpson Scale according to intensity, with wind speed for a one-minute average being the determining factor. The scale was developed in the 1970s by Robert Simpson, a meteorologist and director of the National Hurricane Center, and by Florida consulting engineer Herbert Saffir, so that weather forecasters might estimate potential property damage for coastal areas at or near the point of landfall. Storm surge "values are highly dependent on the slope of the continental shelf in the landfall region."

A Category 1 storm has winds of 74–95 miles per hour, a central barometric pressure of 28.94 inches or more, and a storm surge of 4–5 feet. It usually causes only minimal damage—primarily to unanchored mobile homes, trees and shrubs, and to poorly constructed signs. There may be some coastal road flooding and pier damage. Agnes in 1972 is an example of a Category 1 hurricane.

Georges in 1998 is an example of a Category 2 hurricane, which features winds of 96–110 m.p.h., a pressure of 28.50–28.93, and a storm surge of 6–8 feet. It can cause considerable damage to mobile homes and poorly constructed signs and piers, damage the roofs of buildings, break the moorings of unprotected small craft, and flood low-lying coastal routes. Georges caused some property damage at least as far inland as Hattiesburg, some 70 miles from the Mississippi Coast.

A Category 3 hurricane has winds of 111–130 m.p.h., a pressure of 27.91–28.49, and a storm surge of 9–12 feet. It may cause extensive damage to small residences and utility buildings, destroy mobile homes and poorly constructed signs, damage trees and shrubbery, create battering rams of floating debris, and flood areas several miles inland. Betsy in 1965 is an example of a Category 3 storm.

A Category 4 hurricane brings winds of 131–155 m.p.h., a pressure of 27.17–27.90, and a storm surge of 13–18 feet, and causes extreme damage to mobile homes, signs, trees, and shrubbery, and to the windows, floors, and roofs of small residences near the shore. "Terrain lower than 10 feet above sea level may be flooded, requiring massive evacuation of residential areas as far inland as six miles." The Grand Isle, Louisiana, hurricane of 1909 was among the most powerful and deadly Category 4 storms ever to strike the U.S. mainland, killing more than 350 people.

A Category 5 hurricane has winds greater than 155 m.p.h., a pressure less than 27.17, and a storm surge higher than 18 feet. The result is catastrophic, creating all of the damage from Categories 1–4 plus more to residences, industrial buildings, and "all structures located less than 15 feet above sea level and within 500 yards of shoreline." Massive evacuation is required on low ground within 5-10 miles of shore.

Through 1998, just 23 Atlantic storms had reached the Category 5 level and only nine of those struck land with that intensity. The only three Category 5 storms ever to hit the U.S. mainland were the Florida Keys Labor Day storm of 1935, with a U.S. record low pressure of 26.35 inches; Camille in 1969, with its 200-plus m.p.h. winds and 24-foot storm surge; and Andrew in 1992, with 165 m.p.h. winds and a barometric pressure of 27.23 inches, creating total damages topping $33 billion. "With the exception of Camille, no Category 5 hurricanes have ever existed north of 30 degrees N nor south of 14 degrees N. Camille's path was 28-30 N, 89W." Hurricane Allen in 1980 was the longest-lasting Category 5 storm, reaching Category 5 intensity "three times through the Southern Caribbean and Gulf of Mexico, twice for twenty-four hours duration and the third lasting eighteen hours." But Allen had weakened by the time of U.S. landfall, as did at least 11 other storms that reached Category 5 status at some point in their life cycles.

According to National Hurricane Center statistics, the U.S. mainland experienced 158 hurricane strikes between 1900 and 1996, including 64 major storms (those in Category 3, 4, or 5). The decade of greatest activity was 1940–1949, with 23 hurricanes, including eight major storms. Florida led all states in hurricane activity from

1990 to 1996 with 57 storm strikes, including 24 major storms. Texas was second with 36 strikes and 15 majors, followed in order by Louisiana, 25 and 12; North Carolina, 25 and 11; South Carolina, 14 and 4; Alabama, 10 and 5; New York, 9 and 5; Mississippi, 8 and 6; Connecticut, 8 and 3; Massachusetts, 6 and 2; and Georgia, 5 and 0. The most hurricane-prone coastal counties in the United States are Monroe County, Florida; Dare County, North Carolina; and Galveston County, Texas.

According to Gerrish, the top six deadliest U.S. storms of the twentieth century were the Galveston hurricane of 1900; the Florida hurricane of 1928 at Lake Okeechobee, Category 4, which killed 1,836; the Florida Keys hurricane of 1919, Category 4, 600 lives; the New England hurricane of 1938, Category 3, 600 lives; the Florida Keys Labor Day storm of 1935, Category 5, 408 lives; and Hurricane Audrey in 1957, Category 4, which claimed 390 lives in Louisiana and Texas. Hurricane Camille in 1969, Category 5, ranked eleventh on the list.

Gerrish listed the top six most intense storms as the Florida Keys Labor Day storm of 1935, Category 5, with a barometric pressure of 26.35 inches; Camille, 1969, Category 5, a pressure of 26.84; Andrew, 1992, Category 5, 27.23; Florida Keys, 1919, Category 4, 27.37; Florida, 1928, Category 4, 27.43; and Donna, 1960, Category 4, 27.46.

USA Today cited the top 10 most damaging U.S. hurricanes, normalized to 1995 dollars, as the southeast Florida/Alabama hurricane of 1926, Category 4, $72.3 billion; Andrew, 1992, Category 5, $33.1 billion; southwest Florida, 1944, Category 3, $16.9 billion; New England, 1938, Category 3, $16.6 billion; southeast Florida, 1928, Category 4, $13.8 billion; Betsy, 1965, Category 3, $12.4 billion; Donna, 1960, Category 4, $12.1 billion; Camille, 1969, Category 5, $11 billion; Agnes, 1972, Category 1, $10.7 billion; and Diane, 1955, Category 1, $10.2 billion.

Despite the great technological advancements made in detecting and tracking the killer storms over the years, much about them remains a mystery. Scientists still do not know which clouds will form into a hurricane, nor can meteorologists predict exactly when and where a storm will strike. Fueled on the solar energy of hot tropical oceans, each cyclone develops its own personality. "They are fickle, erratic, headstrong," wrote Jeffrey Rosenfeld in *Eye of the Storm: Inside the World's Deadliest Hurricanes, Tornadoes and Blizzards.*

An early innovator in the study of storms was Benjamin Franklin, who began his experiments with electricity in 1746. His invention of the first electrical conductor, or lightning rod, in 1752 opened the door to the age of meteorology, led to observations and theories based on natural law, and forever changed people's relationship with storms. According to Rosenfeld, "The lightning rod was a huge intuitive leap in science and an ancient dream come true in meteorology. It was a light that brought meteorology out of the dark." Through observation and study, Franklin was able to track the progress of a hurricane from North Carolina to New England in 1749 and "verify his theory that the storm had moved from one place to another." It would be the 1830s, however, before another American hurricane researcher, William Redfield, became the first person to track the path of a hurricane from the West Indies to the U.S. East Coast.

Two centuries before Franklin, in 1643, Evangelista Torricelli, a professor of mathematics in the Florentine Academy, discovered the principle of the barometer, recognizing that its variations were associated with changes in the weather. Barometers indicate the atmospheric pressure by gradient indirectly as the height in inches of a column of mercury, which falls rapidly as the center of a hurricane approaches and as the wind velocity increases. As Ivan Ray Tannehill put it in *Hurricanes*: "The rate of decrease in pressure between two places is known as the 'gradient.' The wind velocity increases with the steepness of the gradient, other things being equal, or as the difference in pressure between the two places increases. Pressure gradients in hurricanes are very steep." The Beaufort Scale, a system of barometric measurements introduced in 1805, allowed sailors to transmit weather observations from sea that "helped to clarify the nature of some rough water events." It was not until the mid-1800s that the invention of the anemometer allowed meteorologists to measure and record wind speeds. Because these instruments are susceptible to getting damaged or lost during intense storms, however, "accurate wind records do not exist for some of the highest winds of the greatest storms."

President Ulysses S. Grant signed a proclamation in 1870 giving the responsibility of gathering weather information, developing weather maps, and issuing storm warnings throughout the nation to the U.S. Army Signal Service. In nearby Cuba, a Jesuit priest named Benito Vines devoted his life to the study of hurricanes, and, before his death in 1893, developed an elaborate warning system throughout the island nation. As Barnes wrote, "He utilized hundreds of volunteer observers, gathered ship reports, issued telegraph warnings to nearby islands and even developed a 'pony express' between isolated villages to warn residents of approaching hurricanes." The U.S. Weather Bureau was created under the Department of Agriculture in 1891, but it was not until the Spanish-American War of 1898 that a comprehensive hurricane forecasting system—forerunner of today's National Hurricane Center—was developed. President William McKinley was said "to have had a greater fear of hurricanes than of attack from the Spanish navy." Because of relatively poor ship-to-shore communications, however, it would be 1909 before the first "in situ" ship report of hurricane conditions was "received in time to assist coastal preparations."

Following a second hurricane at Galveston, Texas, in 1902, the U.S. Weather Bureau moved its hurricane forecast office from Havana, Cuba, to Washington, D.C. The office was moved to Jacksonville, Florida, in 1933 and was moved again in 1943 to Miami, where it was charged with the "responsibility to track and forecast all tropical storms and hurricanes in the Atlantic Ocean, Caribbean Sea and Gulf of Mexico." Today's National Hurricane Center (NHC) is located on the campus of Florida International University in Miami.

Once detected, a hurricane's movement is closely watched and plotted, and Miami's far-reaching hurricane warning system is activated. The center not only acts as a clearinghouse for storm information from that point on, but also coordinates a steady stream of bulletins and advisories to the public. An office in New Orleans also issues bulletins and other storm information within a region covering the western and central Gulf Coast, but Miami handles the rest of the eastern Gulf to New England, where the Boston office takes over. The NHC maintains a continuous watch on tropical cyclones from May 15 through November 30 each year and, during the off-season, provides training for U.S. emergency managers and representatives of other countries affected by the storms. The center also conducts research aimed at improving forecasting techniques and conducts public awareness programs.

Congress grew concerned during the 1940s and 1950s over the growing increase in the number of hurricanes affecting the United States each year and began pumping more money into storm research and new technologies. "It was a simple catastrophic event, however—Hurricane Camille in 1969—which brought these separate efforts and disciplines together in recognition of the multi-faceted nature of the problem," wrote Pielke and Pielke.

Meteorologists and weather forecast services eagerly snapped up each new generation of supercomputers, which in the 1970s began to predict weather as well as or better than the best human forecasters. The NHC maintains about a half-dozen computer models that forecast hurricanes based on historical information and current weather data from inside a storm, as well as making predictions about the changing atmosphere in advance of the storm. Experts monitor the computers to mix human intuition with modern technology.

The European Space Agency's METEOSAT-6 geostationary satellite monitors tropical waves off the African coast and over the tropical North Atlantic. The satellites remain in a fixed position in orbit, in relation to the earth's rotation. The National Oceanic and Atmospheric Administration's satellite system is composed of the Geostationary Operational Environment Satellites (GOES) for national and regional short-range warning, and the Polar-Orbiting Operational Environmental Satellites (POES) for global forecasting and environmental monitoring. In addition, forecasters use data from some 5,000 daily wind readings from jet aircraft and about 4,000 land stations across the globe, thousands of ships and fixed buoys that measure ocean temperatures, and even "perishable balloons released twice daily around the world that sample the upper atmosphere." Enhanced infrared (IR) imagery is used at night. Although most public policy for coping with hurricane threats is reactive, forecasters strive to provide at least 12 daylight hours of warning to a potential strike area. Strength estimates are made using the so-called "Dvorak technique." The method devised by NOAA meterologist Vernon Dvorak in the 1970s utilizes satellite imagery to locate the eye of the hurricane and project its next stage of development.

The National Hurricane Center also includes the Chief, Aerial Reconnaissance Coordination, All Hurricanes (CARCAH) unit—a small, three-person unit of the 53rd Reconnaissance Squadron (Hurricane Hunters)— operating out of Keesler Air Force Base at Biloxi, Mississippi. CARCAH tasks the flying units at the NHC to meet all reconnaissance requirements in the Atlantic and central Pacific areas. The Hurricane Hunters, normally WC-130 aircraft, fly into the center of the storm and transmit data directly to CARCAH via satellite. The data is screened and verified by hurricane specialists for use in the forecast and warning process, then entered into the world weather networks.

The Hurricane Hunters document the precise location of the storm center, the minimum sea level pressure in the center, and the distribution of flight winds in four quadrants about the center. They usually investigate at an altitude of about 1,500 feet above the ocean surface, with NOAA P-3 aircraft serving as backup for the missions. As the storm builds in strength, the aircraft move to higher altitudes. "The ride can get pretty bumpy" and "sometimes the clouds and rain are so thick, the aircraft's wings are barely visible to the crew," according to the article "Hurricane Hunters" by the Federal Emergency Management Agency. The six-member crews of the Hurricane Hunters usually include the aircraft commander, copilot, flight engineer, navigator, weather officer, and a dropsonde system operator. "The dropsonde system operator releases the dropsonde—a weather-sensing canister attached to a small parachute, which transmits radio signals back to the airplane about temperature, humidity, pressure and winds inside the storm," states the FEMA article. That data is forwarded by satellite to the NHC. A new high-altitude NOAA Gulfstream G-IV jet plane now performs hurricane surveillance flight missions at around 40,000 feet. They drop instrument packages called "dropwindsones," which "document vertical profiles of temperature, pressure, moisture and winds at many locations in the environment surrounding the storm . . . three-dimensional data . . . desperately needed to upgrade numerical model performance."

Despite the advances in meteorological techniques over the years, however, forecasters still have trouble determining exactly where a hurricane will make landfall and the level of intensity with which it will strike. The storms tend to move in accordance with the winds, and, as heat-absorbing engines, they gain strength as they pass over warm water. Intensifying storms, to some degree, make their own track, and, reacting to a number of meteorological variables, they can make sudden turns, such as Camille's sharp veers toward the northwest in 1969. Slower-moving hurricanes tend to wobble (called the trochoidal motion) more than faster-moving storms and their course can be greatly affected by collapsing steering currents or approaching troughs. Aircraft observations have shown that hurricanes, as Rosenfeld put it, "stagger in toward landfall like drunks unable to walk the line: they zigzag back and forth. By the end of the 1960s, mathematical models showed that this drunken sway is an oscillation caused not by steering currents, but instead by the internal wobble of the hurricane structure." For these reasons, the intuition, experience, and skills of seasoned hurricane specialists sometimes must supercede technology in determining intensity and predicting landfall.

Although hurricanes are not controllable, their impact can be mitigated by strong prestorm actions, and there is no substitute for common sense in the face of such a threat. As U.S. coastal populations continue to grow—including rising numbers of elderly Americans—evacuations are still an area of primary concern. "With the growth in exposed populations and property . . . proactive policy increasingly is needed to anticipate and mitigate potential risks," wrote Godschalk, Beatley, and Brower.

The warm waters of the U.S. Gulf Coast and proximity to tropical waters make the entire region a "magnet for storms." Large metropolitan areas such as Tampa,

Florida, and New Orleans are particularly vulnerable to the wind and water of tropical storms. Small wonder then that, in June of each year, Catholic churches all across the Gulf Coast hold novenas to Our Lady of Prompt Succor. They are praying for protection against the god of storms—Hunraken.

KILLER CAMILLE

"Get out! Get out!" a voice blared over the loudspeaker of a passing National Guard vehicle. "This is a very dangerous area." The warning echoed through otherwise silent streets as guardsmen combed the beachfront neighborhood around Robert Taylor's Gulfport home. It was just before sundown that Sunday evening of August 17, 1969, but the sun had long been hidden by the dark clouds of the approaching storm. Military and local law enforcement officials were making the rounds in this and other neighborhoods up and down the Mississippi Coast in a frantic effort to get residents to leave before it was too late. But time was running out.

As Camille neared the mouth of the Mississippi River to the west, oil rigs were sent careening off their platforms into the churning waters of the Gulf, and more than 90 vessels of varying size, including some oceangoing ships, ran aground or sank outright. The hurricane surged through the Louisiana marshes, topping levees and destroying everything in its path. At Buras,

Louisiana, formerly a town of 6,000, only six structures were left intact. The storm sideswiped New Orleans with wind gusts of 100 miles an hour and blasted Mobile, Alabama, on the opposite end of the Mississippi Coast with 75-mile-an-hour winds. However, it saved the brunt of its fury—winds of more than 200 miles an hour and a tidal surge of 24 feet—for the Mississippi Gulf Coast over a five-hour period of hell and high water. Camille would be only the third Category 5 storm ever to strike the U.S. mainland and would produce the nation's second-lowest barometric reading at 26.84 inches. America's only other Category 5 storms were the Florida Keys Labor Day hurricane of 1935, with a record-low barometric pressure of 26.35 inches, and Hurricane Andrew in 1992 at 27.23.

Like many other Gulf Coast residents, Taylor and his guests, Billy Barrett and Mary Evelyn Wallace, thought they could ride out the storm in safety. They made sandwiches and flipped on a transistor radio. But instead of monitoring local-station broadcasts, which were warning people to evacuate, they tuned in to New Orleans radio station WWL, which was describing Camille only as a "severe storm." They didn't consider leaving, even though, as nightfall descended, they could see the murky waters of the Gulf already churning over the sandy beach just across U.S. Highway 90.

Westward down the beach at Pass Christian, police chief Gerald Peralta and his three-man crew of officers scurried door to door now in a last-ditch effort to persuade residents to leave. But a lot of the old-timers had ridden out the hurricane of 1947 and, more recently, Betsy in 1965. They weren't budging. At the Dambrink home, John, Sr., (Pops) and Anna (Mother) went to bed about 7:30 p.m., while Elizabeth (Sis) Dambrink made coffee for Piet and Valena Stegenga and Piet's half-brother, John, Jr., (Joey) Dambrink. Meanwhile, wheel-chair-bound Edith de Vries, nursing a fractured hip, huddled with her daughter, Earle, and the four members of the Lafollette family at the de Vries home on Pass Christian's West Beach. In the auditorium of Pass Christian's old Trinity Episcopal Church, Paul Williams tried to relax with his 48-year-old wife, Myrtle, while his children and grandchildren played. At the nearby Richelieu Manor apartment complex, Mary Ann Gerlach and her husband, Fritz, napped in their second-story apartment while some of the other 21 residents who had not evacuated watched the Gulf waters rise over the beach across Highway 90. Ben Duckworth, Richard (Rick) and Luane Keller, the 80-year-old Jack and the wheelchair-bound Zoe Matthews, Mike Gannon, and Mike Bielan gathered in apartment 316, poured a few beers, watched TV, and prayed that the storm would pass them by. Another person described as a woman with brown hair, possibly 26-year-old Shirley Ann Geshke, also joined the group. When it appeared that Camille would veer westward toward Texas, Rick Keller breathed a sigh of relief and retired to a rear bedroom to get some needed rest.

Farther west, past Henderson Point and just across St. Louis Bay, 33-year-old Dr. Henry Maggio busied himself at the local hospital, finding that the work helped assuage his earlier feelings of "impending doom and disaster." Another physician, Dr. Marion Dodson, helped Maggio care for some 50 patients and assist another 200 people who came to the hospital to seek protection from the storm. The refugees lined the hallways and waited. In neighboring Waveland, Alderman Johnny Longo made his final trip around town as winds grew stronger about 8:30 p.m. Then, he joined about 40 friends and relatives who had gathered at his home, located along the railroad tracks about three blocks from the beach. They drank coffee, played checkers, talked, and waited.

Eastward, on the opposite end of the beach, across Biloxi Bay in Ocean Springs, John Switzer watched television with his wife, Avis, their two small sons, John, Jr., nine, and Jimmy, seven, and Avis's mother, Nell, at the Switzer home on Ruskin Avenue, located about 800 feet from the Gulf. The adults had a couple of drinks, laughed and talked, and switched from channel to channel to keep up with storm reports. By 7 p.m., they noticed that the winds were picking up sharply, but they were not particularly worried. The house was built on pilings and had a floor level of 14 feet, equal to the tidal surge of the 1947 storm. Jimmy crawled up on the living room couch and went to sleep as the family relaxed.

"Let's go to the hotel," the youngsters pleaded at Alma Anderson's old home in Biloxi. "You talk Grandma into going and we'll go," Alma replied. Nephew Rocky, six, and niece Wanda, nine, took that as a positive signal. They ran upstairs, packed their suitcases, ran back downstairs and deposited them on the dining room table. But Glennan Anderson's mother, Althea, and the other older folks, all in their 70s, had no intention of going anywhere. They included Roy, a bachelor uncle; Walter, one of Roy's friends, who lived in a nearby trailer park and had come to the Anderson home for safety; and two aunts, including the diminutive Maurice Stella Tucei, who was only four foot eight. Maurice Stella went upstairs to her bedroom, locked her door and, as always before retiring, took off her hearing aid. The shutters outside the windows of the newly remodeled house were noisily flopping around in the intensifying wind. "Aunt Alma," shouted one of the kids. "You better come in here. All this wind is blowing and it's going to ruin your new curtains." Alma thought to herself, "Oh my goodness, I've just put them up and now they are going . . ."

At Biloxi's Broadwater Beach Hotel on Highway 90, 61-year-old golf pro Charles Webb had spent the day boarding up windows and securing course facilities— including the pro-shop apartment where he lived with his wife, Lillian. Together that evening, the couple watched the rising tide across Highway 90 and listened to the snarling howl of the wind. All of a sudden, bam! Nearby electrical transformers blew about 8:15 p.m., and Charles thought it sounded "like one of those 155 millimeter cannons went off out there . . . a terrific noise." Up and down the coast, in a staggered sequence of power outages from community to community, the lights went out, leaving residents groping around in the shadowy illumination of flashlights, candles, and flickering kerosene lamps. TV sets gave way to transistor radios.

At nearby Keesler Air Force Base, located about 10 feet above sea level, Gregory Durrschmidt and his fellow airmen could hear the wind blowing harder about 9:30 p.m. as they lined the first-floor hallway and walls of their barracks with mattresses and put fresh batteries in their flashlights. As airmen from the top two floors joined those on the first floor, the occupants put more mattresses against room windows to stop flying debris and placed extra mattresses nearby to "form sort of a protective tunnel" in case of a roof collapse. In total darkness except for the flashlights, the men waited in silence as the wind continued to increase in intensity. "Only two city blocks of homes and a raised railroad grade" stood between the servicemen and the Gulf of Mexico.

By the time Lois Toomer and her friend and maid, Mary Fitzpatrick, had made the short trip from the Toomer home at Fifteenth Street and Nineteenth Avenue in Gulfport to the home of Lois's older sister on the corner of Burke Avenue and Fifth Street in Long Beach, just west of Gulfport, the power was off and some pine trees had been blown down in neighborhood yards. By 9 p.m., the winds were so bad that Gulfport's Mayor Philip Shaw, headquartered at the local police station, ordered the release of all prisoners from the city jail. Thanks, but no thanks. Not a one would leave. They were not going anywhere, the inmates told their jailers. In jail, they had food and lodging. Outside, they had nothing but the uninviting grasp of the approaching hurricane.

Outside, in the chilly blackness, the killer called Camille gripped her deadly fingers around the eerily deserted streets and beachfront of the Mississippi Gulf Coast. Wade and Julia Guice hunkered down to their jobs at the Harrison County Emergency Operations Center in Gulfport and civil defense office in Biloxi, respectively, trying to maintain lines of communication with key military and civilian officials and rescue workers as telephone and power poles snapped under increasing winds from the sea. In the back of their minds, they worried about the vulnerability of their own home, located just a couple of blocks north of the old Biloxi Lighthouse on U.S. Highway 90, and the safety of their daughter, Judy, whom they had sent to stay with a friend on the north side of Biloxi Bay—a seemingly safe haven where the elevation was 16 feet above sea level. It would be a long night, but at least Judy would be out of harm's way.

The storm, after flirting with New Orleans, aimed its ugly and tightly wound eye at Pass Christian's Henderson Point, sending a 24-foot tide and accompanying 10-foot wave crashing onto the Mississippi shoreline—swirling over the beach and seawall, rolling across Highway 90 and gushing into homes, businesses, churches, and whatever stood in its way, from Lake Shore on the far western end of the Coast to Pascagoula on the east. The 34-foot wall of water and winds clocked at more than 200 miles an hour shattered trees and man-made structures as if they were matchsticks, many buildings simply imploding from the second-lowest barometric pressure recorded in U.S. history.

Forty-year-old Robert Taylor and his guests were mixing drinks about 10 p.m. as the roar of the wind nearly drowned out the weather reports of New Orleans radio personality Nash Roberts. "My feet are getting wet!" Barrett suddenly exclaimed. Simultaneously, they looked down and saw water gurgling in under the kitchen door. "Oh, my God!" yelled Taylor. He ran into the living room, snatched up his new Persian rug, and put it on a sofa to keep it from getting wet. Pointing the beam of his flashlight through a glass door, he saw that the water already was a foot deep and coming into the house. Within seconds, it was knee-deep and rising. Now, it was waist deep, and Taylor's recently purchased encyclopedias were floating into the hall. Crash! There was a sharp noise in the kitchen as the refrigerator overturned, then a louder crash at the dwelling's front entrance. "What was that?" yelled Mary Evelyn. About that time, Taylor's front double doors popped off their hinges and his new Oldsmobile Delta 88 came floating in on the tide. Reacting in desperation, Taylor and Barrett pushed the car back outside in the chest-deep water, then opened its doors so it would sink. It was then that Taylor remembered the electronic equipment from his boat, which he had put into his car trunk that morning to protect it from the storm. So much for safekeeping.

All of a sudden, there was another tidal surge and they were all up to their necks in the Gulf of Mexico. Battered by wind, water, floating furniture, and debris, they noticed that the ceiling was closing in. Frantic, they swam out the front door and grabbed hold of steel rods connecting the house's brick pillars, hanging on for dear life as the storm raged. That's when Taylor looked up and noticed his "neighbor's kitchen floating down Alfonso Drive." Another two-story house on the beach was now a one-story house. Everything seemed to be happening in slow motion. One house disintegrated. Then, an empty boat came floating down the street. The trio briefly considered making a swim for the boat, but the air and water were filled with debris, driven like machine-gun bullets by the shrieking winds. Not a good move. "Something's around my leg," gasped Taylor, fearing that snakes had been washed up from the bayous. He breathed a sigh of relief as the "snake" turned out to be a flyline from one of his fishing rods. Taylor and his friends hung onto the steel rods and to each other as they watched the interior walls of Taylor's home collapse. The red glow of the sky above them came from a neighbor's home, which had caught fire two blocks away. Taylor grabbed a floating chair to shield himself and his friends from dangerous floating debris.

Shining a flashlight out into the pitch black night, John Switzer watched rising water from the draw located behind his Ocean Springs home climb about halfway up a four-foot fence that separated his house from that of neighbor Andy Anderson. About 10 p.m., he began to have serious second thoughts about the wisdom of riding out the hurricane in their exposed position so near the Gulf. Everyone in the Switzer household was on edge. They knew if the water flooded the street and driveway, the only way out would be to walk or swim. Switzer ventured out onto a little concrete step outside the front door and stepped down into water. "It hasn't rained that much," he thought. He dipped a finger into the water and inserted it into his mouth, and was startled by the taste of salt. By now, the rising water had nearly reached the top of the border fence out in the darkness. "Let's go!" Switzer yelled. The family started scurrying around, grabbing things to take with them. "We don't have time!" warned John. "Get in the car!" Quickly, they packed up the kids and two cats, grabbed a couple of blankets, and headed for their cars. Then, on second thought, John let the cats loose outside to fend for themselves.

Nell, clutching her prize coin collection, got behind the wheel of her own car. Avis drove one of the Switzer cars and John the other. Forming a three-vehicle caravan, they swerved past falling heavy oak and pecan tree limbs, onto sidewalks, dodging and weaving, making haste for the downtown bank where John worked. Sheet metal and corrugated tin from a nearby lumberyard sailed through the air all around them, bouncing and crumpling as it hit the ground or other objects. John thought the wind was "screaming like a banshee," a high-pitched scream as gusts would blow past the fleeing family. Finally, they reached the bank shortly after 11 p.m. and got inside. Wet, weary, and scared, they huddled inside as wind and water pelted the glass doors of the bank's front entrance. Except for young Jimmy, they were too nervous to sleep. Jimmy had slept through it all.

At the Broadwater Beach Hotel golf course in Biloxi, Charles and Lillian Webb fought for their lives as Camille plowed through their pro-shop apartment like Attila the Hun at a garden party. One crash after another and then, bam! Something hit a wall and in gushed the water. A television set floated through from the living room to the bedroom as the waves dashed against the complex. Then, the refrigerator floated over a collapsing wall. Charles clutched a flashlight in his right hand. Reaching under the waves with his left hand, he pulled Lillian up out of the water and debris. Finally, they climbed out of the water to the relative safety of a window ledge, where "Lillian stood up there and prayed for the whole time" the storm was at its worst. Eastward down Highway 90, at the beachfront Buena Vista Hotel, WLOX radio announcer Richard Shultz determinedly clung to his microphone as the hurricane sent a big wave smashing into the building's arcade and broadcast studio. At exactly 10:03 p.m., listeners still tuned into transistor radios heard Shultz sign off "amid the sounds of shattering glass and bumping furniture." Time to abandon shift.

A "terrifying, angry shriek" announced Camille's arrival at Keesler Air Force Base, a "deafening scream" that, to Durrschmidt and his fellow airmen, seemed to "come from everywhere." The sound of crashing glass and other debris was momentarily interrupted by another noise, "like thousands of bullets striking the outer concrete walls." Camille was sucking up stones from base rooftops and spitting them back with contempt. With the aid of flashlights, the soldiers watched torrents of wind-driven rain blast down stairwells and gush underneath the doors, flooding the lower floor. Durrschmidt, standing motionless with his back against a wall, felt helpless and trapped, cut off from the rest of the world. A "wave of fear" crashed over him as he realized he might die in the storm. The cement-block building began to "throb rhythmically from the pounding, wind, water and flying debris." In the darkness, someone sobbed uncontrollably. Then, one airman panicked and tried to flee. Durrschmidt watched the "brief scuffle as the screaming airman was tackled and held down" by fellow soldiers, for his own safety. The men then formed a "bucket brigade" in a vain attempt to stem the flow of water into the barracks, but abandoned the effort when it appeared that the roof might collapse. They took shelter within the seemingly safer confines of their mattress tunnel, huddling together as the storm engulfed the base.

Alma Anderson, just a week away from her 42nd birthday, was still preoccupied with saving the window curtains of her sturdy and just-remodeled home in Biloxi. The electricity was out, but kerosene lamps burned in four rooms. By flashlight, Alma noticed water seeping in around the carpet near her front door. "The wind is blowing the [rain] water underneath the carpet," she thought. First the curtains and now the carpet. What next? Then, she shined the light through the glass door onto the front porch and saw sloshing waves. "Oh, dear God," she exclaimed. "That's not rain! The water is on the front porch and is coming into the house!" She shouted the alarm to Glennan, who was upstairs checking on a collapsing chimney. "What the heck do you want?" he yelled back. "We've got to get the heck out of here," Alma replied. "Water is coming into the house. The waves are on the porch." Glennan scurried down the stairs to take a look, then darted back up the stairway to alert the old folks. He banged on Aunt Maurice Stella Tucei's locked bedroom door, but couldn't get an answer, so he broke it down. Then, he rousted Walter, Roy, and the other aunt. Finally, everyone, including the two kids, was downstairs.

By this time, about 10 p.m., the water was gushing into the house. They opened the back door to let the water through and Alma caught a glimpse of the family car floating down the street. At that point, she would have gladly traded the Cadillac for a canoe. The youngsters, panic-stricken, were crying, and Alma muttered to herself, "Oh dear God, we are trapped in this house. Let me make it to the telephone!" Amazingly, the phone line was still working and Alma called Biloxi police, but no one was available to come to the rescue. Suddenly, there was a large crashing sound as the front part of the Anderson house blew away and jammed up against the structure's interior staircase, preventing escape to a higher floor for all except Walter, who had made it upstairs in the nick of time. With water up to their hips, the family waded into the kitchen and clung to the sink as other appliances and furniture washed through the room. "Aunt Alma, save us," pleaded one of the kids. Alma thought, "Dear God, these children think I can save them. I can't even save myself. I can't swim!" Then, she tried to soothe them. "We'll do something, hon," she said. "Just don't cry." But then, the house began to crumble, wall by wall, and they were all blown out into the terrifying darkness. Alma and Aunt Maurice Stella went under, but Glennan pulled them up. "If you can find a board or anything to hang onto, hang onto it," he yelled. "If you've got a board, you won't go under." But the waves were getting rougher by the minute.

Alma went under again and Glennan pulled her back up. She grabbed hold of a piece of floating lumber just as a tidal wave hit. Under water, back up. Under water, back up. Alma swallowed salt water and gasped for breath. "Oh dear God," she thought. "They say what you're most scared of, that's the way you're going [to die]. I've been scared of water all my life and this is it. I'm going and I don't want to die. There is so much I'd like to do. God, if you'll just let me live and let me get these kids to safety, there is so much I'd like to do . . . Nobody can save me but God himself. If he will just hear me this one time, I will be satisfied." She thought about her mother: "If I could just tell her how much I loved her." Under water, back up.

Under water, back up. Finally, exhausted, she felt her energy slipping away. Just about to give up the fight for life, she saw a vision, "just like through the Lord," and seemed to hear a voice telling her, "When you go under, hold your breath, when you come up, breathe." Now, Alma saw what appeared to be the face of one of her beauty salon customers, Barbara Fewill. "I can see Barbara's face," she thought, as the vision faded away. Then, back to reality, she saw Glennan up ahead, waving a flashlight and yelling. For an instant, she spotted little Rocky's "cotten hair" and nearly panicked when she saw a board with a nail in it floating straight for the youngster. She reached out to grab the board, but a big wave caught it and turned it harmlessly away. Then, she heard Glennan again, yelling out names. One by one, members of the Anderson household answered—except for the two elderly aunts.

At the hospital in Bay St. Louis, the power went out about 9 p.m., but emergency generators kicked in to keep everything functioning for patients and storm refugees alike. Maggio and Dodson calmly went about their duties as they watched the rising waters from a nearby bayou climb up the first step and then the second step of the medical facility, which was elevated about four feet off the ground. With pinecones whizzing through the air "like bazooka shells," another off-duty physician and his son walked and crawled their way from their nearby home to the hospital during the height of the storm. Maggio was shocked by the appearance of his refugee colleague—who seemed to be physically and emotionally traumatized by the ordeal—and thought the doctor had "aged 10 years." Suddenly, about 11 p.m., the wind stopped blowing and the trees stood still. Maggio walked outside and, to his amazement, the sky was clear and calm. The eye of Camille was passing. It lasted about 15 minutes, then the winds started again from the opposite, counterclockwise direction. With the low barometric pressure, the eye had sucked up water. Now, it was dumping it back on the Mississippi Coast with a vengeance. In Waveland, Longo also noticed: "The barometric pressure was low and the volume of water that had been drawn up into the eye of the hurricane [was so great that it] let loose as the eye came on shore and completely flooded the area all the way up to the railroad track"—a dead calm and then the water came.

At Long Beach, located between Pass Christian and Gulfport, Lois Toomer looked out the south window of her sister's home, one block off the beach, and saw that the rising water had reached the level of the windowsill. Five feet! A boat floated by, upside down. "God is in this house," Lois thought to herself. "It's a sign. Don't try to go outside." The 56-year-old Meridian native forgot about the crippling bursitis in her left hip and began bouncing around with a spunkiness that belied her age and medical condition. Water spewed through the floor furnace like a geyser. The bathroom commode suddenly was uprooted and the house was flushed from its foundation. Quickly, the women found themselves wading though waist-deep water. "Mrs. Toomer, this house is mooooooving!" screamed Mary. Lois was scared spitless. Her mouth was so dry she couldn't swallow, much less spit. Her crippled sister, who had to use a cane to get around, was in a daze. Mary picked up the household Bible with one hand and grabbed a hammer with the other. Heaven in one hand, resolution in the other, hellbent to survive. An antique, drop-leaf table came floating by. It looked like a ship to the women and they grabbed hold. Mary dropped the hammer and began reading aloud from the Bible. A credenza floated by and Lois thought about lunging for the bigger ship. "God, what should we do?" she muttered, with head bowed and eyes closed. "Should we go to the credenza?" Then, she opened her eyes as the credenza overturned. "Thank you, Lord," she said. "You have given me my sign. We were not supposed to go there."

But what now? Lois wondered. Mary provided the answer. "Mrs. Toomer, get down on your knees, woman." The women got down on their knees in the water and prayed for deliverance. "God, please forgive me for putting other things first and I'll never forget you," prayed Lois. "Please give me a chance and guide me for the rest of my life." When they finished and stood up, Mary, hallucinating, looked directly at Lois and cried, "Lord, God, you done sent my mama to me. Oh, Lord God, how glad I am to see my mama!" Lois thought Mary had flipped, but played along. "Yes, little Mary," she said. "You are all right. Mama's here." Lois's sister said nothing. Holding a kerosene lamp, Lois prayed again, to herself, for a sign from God. Then, all of a sudden, there was a sharp scraping noise. The limbs of a magnolia tree were brushing against a window. That was Lois's sign. The magnolia tree was located north of the house. If the house was moving north, at least the tide wasn't reversing itself and sweeping them southward, out into the Gulf—Lois's greatest fear. She rejoiced in the revelation while her sister observed that "Lois is going crazy." Mary held up the Bible to keep it from getting wet. Weak from fright, the three women prayed together: "Let this pass from us."

In Pass Christian, the 38-year-old Peralta and his fellow police officers were forced to abandon their patrol cars about 9 p.m. because of the rapidly rising water and snarling wind. The chief posted his officers at the police station on Second Street and obtained an amphibious LARC vehicle that had been provided to the Harrison County supervisor's office by the Mississippi Army National Guard. About 10 p.m., as Camille began to unleash the full brunt of her fury, Peralta, one civilian, and four National Guardsmen piled into the LARC and proceeded to maneuver the vehicle up and down Second Street to provide help wherever they could. With the streets now under water and unavailable for escape, they heard screams for help coming from the trapped residents of a nearby house. Facing an unrelenting wind, one of the rescuers dived overboard with a rope and tied the LARC to a tree. Then, the men pulled the LARC to the tree. They repeated the maneuver several times until they reached the house and rescued its occupants. After dropping the waterlogged refugees off at the city's nearby Catholic school, Peralta and crew continued their rescue efforts—pulling people out of attics, out of trees, out of the water—as the storm continued to rage into the late night and early morning hours. At one house, they had to bulldoze a fence with the LARC in order to rescue the residents. Tornadoes spinning off from the hurricane tore tin from houses and other buildings and sent the deadly sheets ripping through the swirling night air. The flames from several burning houses lent a scary red glow to Mother Nature's madness and mayhem. Peralta peered into the flame-lit waters that inundated the old Gulf-front city and saw the reddish outline of a peculiar-looking object beneath the surface. It was a red Ford Mustang. "Somebody sure lost a pretty car," he thought.

Wheelchair-bound Edith de Vries flinched when she heard the crash of glass windows on the porch of her 50-year-old beachfront home in Pass Christian about 10 p.m. As she, daughter Earle, and the four Lafollettes retreated to a rear bedroom, water gurgled into the house under the front door. The water rose higher and higher, floating iron furniture from the porch and posts from the piers across Highway 90 into and through the house. Out of her wheelchair now, Edith was standing inside a bedroom closet, bracing herself with a walker. Walls cracked, mirrors and pictures fell, and the ceiling was closing in on the trapped inhabitants as the room filled with water, floating furniture, and debris. As the ceiling began breaking up, two of the Lafollettes pushed a hole through to the roof from a bathroom and started pulling the others out. The 52-year-old Earle—a former ballet and tap dancer who had once performed for England's Queen Mother—was pulled out first and was immediately blown off the roof into the water. She went under, then back up, then under again, then back up—finally saving herself by catching onto the trunk of an uprooted pine tree.

The Lafollette family managed to stay together on a roof section as it floated about 200 feet to more shallow water near a rental cottage, where three other residents survived. Meanwhile, Edith Byrd de Vries, 73 at the time, had the wildest ride of her life as she was blown off the roof and into the debris-filled water. Grabbing hold of floating lumber from the disintegrating house, she sailed it—without benefit of paddle or rudder—past the carport, past the Lafollette cottage, past her daughter's studio, and past the other brick rental cottage, amazingly without banging into any of them. The waves transported her in a northwesterly direction, over the railroad tracks a quarter of a mile away and into a grove of small pine trees beyond, where her "boat" became lodged in a jam of other debris. Drenched and chilled to the bone, worried about snakes, she settled uncomfortably onto her makeshift island, much of which had been her house.

Shortly before 10 p.m., Anna Dambrink awoke from her sleep as Valena Stegenga and Sis brought a cup of hot coffee to her bedroom. A lighted candle on a closet shelf provided illumination, but the telephone was still working and suddenly it rang. It was Piet and Valena's grown son calling from California. "Mama, how is the weather over there?" he asked. "Well, it's getting rough," she replied. "Well, y'all be careful and try not to let anything happen," he said. He talked to Sis for a few minutes, and then the phone line went dead. All of a sudden, there was water on the floor and Valena thought it was rain blowing up under the front door. Sis, Piet, and Joey were in the kitchen, and Pops and Mother Dambrink were still in bed. Momentarily stunned, Valena sat there, without saying a word, and watched the water seep into the bedroom. By now, however, everyone realized the danger. Piet and Joey grabbed the TV set and put it up on a counter as the water rose. Pops yelled for help, and Piet and Sis were trying to get to him, but a chair had become lodged in the hallway and was blocking their way. Finally, they got to Pops and began taking him out. Meanwhile, Valena and Joey went into the bedroom after Mother Dambrink. But the house was quickly filling with water and the mattress on the bed was floating toward the ceiling. "Joey, make a hole in the roof," cried Valena. Instead, Joey took his stepmother in his arms and started moving toward the hallway. "Mother, hold tight and don't let go of me," said Joey. Valena followed toward the hallway, but the water was now over her head. "Oh, Joey, I can't swim!" she yelled. Then, biting her tongue, she thought to herself, "Oh my goodness, what am I saying? I can't tell him that. He's got Mother in his arms. He can't let her go to help me." She grabbed hold of anything that would float as she struggled for her life in the crumbling house.

Meanwhile, Piet struggled with Pops. He tried to lift him up out of the water and put him on top of Sis's parked car, but something tore Pops from his arms and the old man disappeared beneath the waves. Now, Piet fought for his own life. Swimming and pushing through the flotsam, he came upon a big pile of floating debris and climbed aboard. It was as good as a boat and he settled into the mishmash of lumber and trash. Then, crack! The devil wind split a nearby telephone pole. "Popped it off like a match, just like you'd cut it with a knife," thought Piet. "Gee whiz! If that pole had fallen on me, I'd be a gone duck." He floated on the trash pile for thirty or forty minutes before he heard somebody hollering, "Save me! Save me!" Piet peered out through the darkness. "Where you at?" he yelled, thinking it was Sis, another nonswimmer in the family. "Sis, I'm coming," Piet yelled again, as he crawled over brush and nail-laden debris toward the sound of the voice. Then, he saw Valena. It was his wife, not Sis. He pulled her onto the trash pile, then grabbed a large piece of floating plywood, which they used to fend off the brutal wind and driving rain. "We must be 10 miles from home," Piet thought, sadly pondering the fate of the rest of the family.

At 120-year-old Trinity Episcopal Church, death also washed in with the tide.

"Papa, the water is coming in!" exclaimed an excited Nick, Paul Williams's son-in-law. The shout awakened the dozing Williams, who jumped up and ran to the front door of the church auditorium, only to find it blocked.

Satellite photo of Camille on August 16, 1969, one day before it struck the Mississippi Gulf Coast (NOAA)

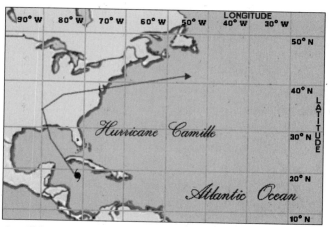

Camille's path of destruction through the southeastern United States (NOAA)

Camille sparked deadly flooding along the James River in Virginia, including the old Confederate capital at Richmond. (NOAA photo/courtesy of the *Richmond Times Dispatch*)

Baricev's Seafood Harbor before (top) and after (bottom) Hurricane Camille (Chauncey Hinman)

Richelieu Apartments before Hurricane Camille (Chauncey Hinman)

Richelieu Apartments after Hurricane Camille (Chauncey Hinman)

Trinity Episcopal Church before (top) and after (bottom) Hurricane Camille (Chauncey Hinman)

The late Paul Williams, pictured here on August 16, 1989, lost thirteen of sixteen family members when Camille demolished historic Trinity Episcopal Church in Pass Christian. (Courtesy of the *Sun Herald*)

St. Stanislaus school on the south beach in Bay St. Louis before Camille. The impressive brick-and-stone, two-story structure was the oldest private boys school in the area. One building housed a bell tower that rose above the two nearby buildings. (Bob Hubbard, Waveland, Mississippi. From the Bob Hubbard Hurricane Camille Photographs, McCain Library and Archives, University of Southern Mississippi)

St. Stanislaus school after Camille, taken from the same angle as the earlier photo. The school has lost its bell tower, sand has washed up over the street, and surrounding trees and branches are broken. (Bob Hubbard, Waveland, Mississippi. From the Bob Hubbard Hurricane Camille Photographs, McCain Library and Archives, University of Southern Mississippi)

A frontal view of the Pirate House on the beach in Waveland before Camille, where live oaks stood in the landscaped yard of the French Colonial structure. (Bob Hubbard, Waveland, Mississippi. From the Bob Hubbard Hurricane Camille Photographs, McCain Library and Archives, University of Southern Mississippi)

The Pirate House from approximately the same angle after Camille, with nothing left except for a metal fence post, some barren and broken trees, and crumbled stone steps leading to a crater where the house had stood for 167 years. (Bob Hubbard, Waveland, Mississippi. From the Bob Hubbard Hurricane Camille Photographs, McCain Library and Archives, University of Southern Mississippi)

The Kimbus home, located on St. Charles Avenue in Bay St. Louis, before Camille. This photo depicts the front and left side of the three-story stucco house that belonged to the Kimbus family. Just prior to this photo being taken, the family had added a hurricane-proof carport and stone wall surrounding a front yard full of oaks. (Bob Hubbard, Waveland, Mississippi. From the Bob Hubbard Hurricane Camille Photographs, McCain Library and Archives, University of Southern Mississippi)

Kimbus home after Camille. Only the hurricane-proof carport and stone wall were left standing, with trees broken and barren. (Bob Hubbard, Waveland, Mississippi. From the Bob Hubbard Hurricane Camille Photographs, McCain Library and Archives, University of Southern Mississippi)

Biloxi's landmark Buena Vista motel, August 19, 1969 (Fred Hutchings, The Hurricane Camille Photograph Collection, McCain Library and Archives, University of Southern Mississippi)

The Confederate Inn Motel in Gulfport, August 20, 1969 (Fred Hutchings, The Hurricane Camille Photograph Collection, McCain Library and Archives, University of Southern Mississippi)

Biloxi's Church of the Redeemer, August 19, 1969 (Fred Hutchings, The Hurricane Camille Photograph Collection, McCain Library and Archives, University of Southern Mississippi)

St. Thomas Catholic Church in Long Beach, August 1969 (Fred Hutchings, The Hurricane Camille Photograph Collection, McCain Library and Archives, University of Southern Mississippi)

Ships washed ashore at the Gulfport harbor, August 1969 (Fred
Hutchings, The Hurricane Camille Photograph Collection,
McCain Library and Archives, University of Southern Mississippi)

The *Wayde Klein* washed up near the Church of the Redeemer in
Biloxi; photo taken August 19, 1969. (Fred Hutchings, The Hurri-
cane Camille Photograph Collection, McCain Library and
Archives, University of Southern Mississippi)

Looking north along Beachfront Drive in Bay St. Louis, August 1969
(Fred Hutchings, The Hurricane Camille Photograph Collection,
McCain Library and Archives, University of Southern Mississippi)

A chair rests along the
shoreline at Long Beach,
August 1969. (Fred Hutch-
ings, The Hurricane
Camille Photograph Col-
lection, McCain Library
and Archives, University
of Southern Mississippi)

The vicinity of 418 West Beach Boulevard in Pass Christian,
August 1969 (Fred Hutchings, The Hurricane Camille Photograph
Collection, McCain Library and Archives, University of Southern
Mississippi)

A tire hanging from a tree, a chair, and a walkway to nowhere, near Waveland Avenue in Bay St. Louis, August 1969 (Fred Hutchings, The Hurricane Camille Photograph Collection, McCain Library and Archives, University of Southern Mississippi)

"Cold 6 packs to go, $1.70": A collapsed house near Lameuse in Biloxi, August 19, 1969 (Fred Hutchings, The Hurricane Camille Photograph Collection, McCain Library and Archives, University of Southern Mississippi)

This drum floated one and a half miles to the intersection of U.S. Highway 90 and 38th Avenue in Gulfport, August 1969. (Fred Hutchings, The Hurricane Camille Photograph Collection, McCain Library and Archives, University of Southern Mississippi)

Looking west along Service Drive in the Pass Christian business district, with city hall and flag flying in the background, August 1969 (Fred Hutchings, The Hurricane Camille Photograph Collection, McCain Library and Archives, University of Southern Mississippi)

The business district of Bay St. Louis after Camille, August 1969
(Fred Hutchings, The Hurricane Camille Photograph Collection,
McCain Library and Archives, University of Southern Mississippi)

National Guardsmen "watching TV" in downtown Gulfport, with
a sailboat in the background, August 19, 1969 (Fred Hutchings,
The Hurricane Camille Photograph Collection, McCain Library
and Archives, University of Southern Mississippi)

Looking north from the beach at the intersection of U.S. Highway 90 and U.S. 49 in Gulfport (Fred Hutchings, The Hurricane Camille Photograph Collection, McCain Library and Archives, University of Southern Mississippi)

Someone is parked in the district attorney's space in downtown Gulfport, August 19, 1969. (Fred Hutchings, The Hurricane Camille Photograph Collection, McCain Library and Archives, University of Southern Mississippi)

"We Shall Overcome," a sign at Pass Christian Isles, August 1969
(Fred Hutchings, The Hurricane Camille Photograph Collection,
McCain Library and Archives, University of Southern Mississippi)

Julia Guice holds three roses
during an August 17, 1998,
ceremony at Gulfport's
Evergreen Forest Cemetery
honoring "Faith, Hope, and
Charity," three unidentified
victims of Camille who are
buried there. (Courtesy of
the *Sun Herald*)

Immediately, he went to the hallway, pulled down the folding stairway to the attic, and started herding his family to the roomy storage area, about 10 to 12 feet above the ground floor. "The floor is doing like fish scales," Williams thought. The concrete rear portion of the building was tightly sealed, meaning the water had nowhere to go but up—and it was rising quickly, tumbling over chairs and tables. "Daddy, Daddy, what are we going to do?" pleaded one of the youngsters. But just as Williams started to pull himself into the attic behind the others, he heard the snap of cracking lumber and everything went blank. Semiconscious, Williams experienced the strange sensation of flying through the air on a piece of kitchen linoleum and landing in water 100 feet away. Kicking and gasping for air, he was washed northward into nearby Live Oak Cemetery. Unable to swim, he luckily boated a passing tree limb, which then slammed into a big oak tree. The caretaker quickly jumped off the limb and into the fork of the tree, which he bear-hugged as the wind and rain whipped his face and body in the sinister darkness of disaster. Perched in the tree, he prayed to God and yelled for help. The church, auditorium, and rectory were gone now, and so were most of his family. Fred DeMetz, a 66-year-old carpenter, was huddling with family and some neighbors in his nearby home as the storm raged, watching "whole sections of houses, whole iceboxes from markets and things passing there like boats in a regatta." He heard screams in the cemetery behind his house as the Trinity church and annexed buildings disintegrated. Then, DeMetz saw the bodies of the Williams family mingle with several freshly buried coffins, airtight boxes, which washed up out of their graves under the intense pressure of the rolling waves. A grisly sight.

Nearby, on the second floor of the Richelieu, Mary Ann Gerlach woke up to banging noises and the violent shaking of the building about the same time Rick Keller was jolted from his nap up in apartment 316. Keller joined his 24-year-old wife, Luane, and the others in the living room. It was getting close to 10 p.m. Ben Duckworth, getting more worried by the minute, began walking downstairs to see how high the water had risen. He opened the stairway door leading outside and shined his flashlight into the pitch black night, only to see the reflection from water just inches below. Downstairs, Mary Ann awakened Fritz. "Hey, somebody's downstairs," she said. "Do you think someone's broken in or something?" They left their bed and walked down the hallway of the shotgun apartment, through the kitchen to the living room, where Mary Ann was startled to see the Gulf waters below and the small panes of the apartment's picture window, boarded on the outside, about to burst from the sinking barometric pressure within. They grabbed some food, retreated back to the bedroom, and shut the door. Then, pop, pop, pop! The windows burst and the water began rushing in. "Come help me!" shouted Fritz, as they put their backs to the bedroom door in a futile effort to stop the water. It was too late. The next thing Mary knew, her bed was floating halfway to the ceiling and the walls were cracking. "Well, I know I'm going to die," she told Fritz. "But I'm not going to die in here with that [third] floor coming down and squashing us." But Fritz couldn't swim, so Mary frantically blew up one of the little rafts she had used in the apartment swimming pool. "You take hold of this because I can swim pretty good," she said, taking a foam-rubber pillow for herself. "I'm going to take the flashlight with me." Fritz, however, didn't budge. He grabbed Mary's arm. "Please, baby, please don't go out! Stay here with me," he begged. "No, I'm going to swim out," she responded, and did so.

Up in 316, Duckworth nervously drank a sip of coffee. He sat his coffee cup down and walked over to Zoe Matthews, sitting in a wheelchair, and put his arm around her. "Will we survive this?" she asked. Duckworth tried to comfort the elderly woman, then looked at his watch. It was 11:14 p.m. That's when the Richelieu and all hell broke loose. There was a sharp sizzling sound of Sheetrock splitting, "like a zipper," and the crash of breaking windows as the salt water poured in. The ceiling cracked, and Duckworth experienced a surreal "slow elevator ride down" as the building crumbled backwards. Thinking quickly, Duckworth and Gannon pried the ceiling studs apart, pushed out the decking, and created an escape hole. Gannon pulled Zoe Matthews from her wheelchair, put her on his back and climbed through the hole. Elderly Jack Matthews made no attempt to leave. As soon as Gannon's head popped through the hole, however, he was sucked out by the 200-plus-mile-an-hour winds and thrown into the raging tide, where he was able to cling to a tree. Zoe Matthews was not so lucky. She was ripped from the Seabee's arms and disappeared. Her body was never found. The Kellers clung to each other as they went out, praying, but death also pulled his beloved Luane from Rick's arms. Shirley Ann Geshke and 39-year-old William Howard Covington also died in the building's collapse, along with Merwin and Helen Jones, raising the Richelieu death toll to at least eight. In the turmoil, Rick saved himself only by latching onto a tree limb. Bielan also survived. As Duckworth emerged through the escape hole, he too was sucked out by the wind and tossed into the water. He was pulled under the tide, then slammed into the long limb of an uprooted, sprawling live oak as he surfaced. Gasping for breath and clawing for survival, he climbed into the tree and buried his face in the grooves of its bark, holding on for dear life.

Meanwhile, Mary Ann Gerlach became entangled in telephone wires and power lines as she was swept into the darkness, but managed to free herself. With the aid of her flashlight, she watched helplessly as Fritz was washed out of the apartment. "Help me, save me!" he cried out, then sank beneath the waves. Struggling for her own life, Mary Ann could see the silhouettes of people on the third floor and the glow of kerosene lanterns disappearing as the building slowly collapsed in the onslaught of wind and water. Swept along in the floating debris, she saw other flickering lights and heard screams, sometimes only 10 or

15 feet away. Then the lights, apparently flashlights, and voices would go away. People were dying all around her. "Oh Lord, if you'll just let me live, I'll try to be a better person," she prayed, using her legs to push through debris from the demolished apartment complex. Swimming and floating on anything that offered relief, Mary Ann was washed beyond the railroad tracks a quarter of a mile north of the beach and into a mountain of debris in a grove of trees. Bleeding from a knee that had been shredded by nails, she took off her bra and used it as a tourniquet. Dressed only in shorts and a short-sleeved sweatshirt to protect her against the chilling wind and rain, she passed out. Gone was the diamond watch Fritz had given her for their second wedding anniversary. Gone was Fritz. Gone was the Richelieu.

When the water started receding about 1 a.m., it went out with a rush. Robert Taylor and his friends—bruised and battered, but otherwise uninjured—held tightly to the steel rods to keep from being pulled out into the Gulf. They huddled in the slime and muck until the first rays of dawn, when Robert realized his Gulfport home had been completely gutted by the storm. The normally scenic and serene beachfront neighborhood in the Second Street area around his home was demolished. It reminded him of the bombed-out cities he had seen during his military service in Korea nearly two decades earlier. He would find out later that his beautiful oceangoing sloop, *Morgan 34*, had disappeared, never to be found. Luckily at the moment, however, a half-full bottle of

Courvoisier came floating by as the tide receded. Barrett speared it, and within seconds the cognac bottle was emptied.

The John Switzer family rode out the storm in the Ocean Springs bank with no injuries. Jimmy was still sleeping when the dawn came, and there was no hysteria until Avis saw the remains of their two-year-old home later that morning. It was a shambles. The roof was gone and there was five feet of water in the house. The brick veneer was blown off the south and west walls of the dwelling, along with the veneer of the family's once-imagined invulnerability. John had just bought a new recliner the previous Friday and it had been delivered that Saturday. The recliner was gone, but the bill remained. Next door, across the four-foot fence, neighbor Andy Anderson and his wife and two kids were still hiding in the attic of their home, tired and traumatized, but uninjured. They had waited too long to flee and were trapped there all night.

Still floating in the debris-filled water in Biloxi, Alma Anderson spotted a flashing light down the street, where a two-story house had become a one-story house. She and other survivors began to scream for help. Quickly, a couple of servicemen from Keesler Air Force Base came to their rescue—pulling Alma, Glennan, Althea, the two youngsters, Uncle Roy, and his friend, Walter, from the wreckage all around them. "Oh Lord, I've been a mean son of a bitch all of my life, but I'm scared to go," Walter murmured, over and over. With cuts and abrasions all over their bodies, stripped of their identification and most of their clothing, the survivors were transported to the Keesler hospital for treatment. "I believe your toe is gone," a medical assistant told Alma. "Well, I believe part of it is still there," asserted Alma, still in shock and pleading for something to quench her terrible thirst. There was no water, nothing to drink. Physicians sewed her toe back onto her foot and gave her a tetanus shot to help ward off infection. Suffering an adverse physiological reaction to the shot, she was still too numb to cry, emotionally and physically drained. The Anderson home was gone—flat as a pancake, nothing left but the doorsteps leading to nowhere. The two aunts were still missing. Then, over the next couple of days, rescue workers noticed a cat returning to the same debris pile and decided to investigate. What they found was heartbreaking. Pulling away some boards from the pile, they saw a hand protruding from the debris. They had found the bodies of the two aunts.

At the Broadwater Hotel, Charles and Lillian Webb survived Camille in their gutted apartment, but the popular Biloxi golf course was devastated. Some 1,500 trees were destroyed or heavily damaged, as were the cart shed and about 80 carts. "When you take a tree a foot and a half in diameter and 100 feet long and you bend that thing over at a 45-degree angle, you've done damaged the tree," Charles would say later, in a bit of understatement. The Buena Vista Hotel also was ruined. Baricev's Restaurant and the Biloxi strip's popular Fiesta Club, where U.S. Airman Gregory Durrschmidt had enjoyed the "slow and easy southern lifestyle," were demolished along with most everything on the beach side of Highway 90. Durrschmidt and his buddies had weathered the storm in the safer confines of Keesler Air Force Base.

As the storm waters receded in Long Beach, Lois Toomer, her older sister, and her friend and maid, Mary Fitzpatrick, sat down in three old rocking chairs, gifts from Lois's mother-in-law. Still dazed, they rocked—and as they rocked, they sang several familiar church hymns: "Master, the Tempest Is Raging," "Peace, Peace Be Still," and "Love Lifted Me." Lois's voice rang out loud and clear: "When nothing else could help, love lifted me." She paused momentarily, then turned to the others and said, "That was Jesus's love lifting us." One by one, they fell asleep. At daylight, there was a sharp banging on the front door as civil defense workers arrived. The editor of the local weekly newspaper later told Lois, "You know, many people died drunk that night . . . You turned to the right person. That's why you're here." Mrs. Toomer said, "It was worth that night to find Jesus." Later, she recorded her Camille experience in a book entitled *Miracle of the Magnolias.*

Rising water finally knocked out the generator of the Bay St. Louis hospital about 1 a.m., but, by that time, most of the patients were medically stabilized and asleep. In Waveland, Alderman Johnny Longo and his group of refugees had survived the storm. However, his house, situated 22 feet above sea level, was flooded with four feet of water. Surveying the damage in Bay St. Louis in the early morning light, Henry Maggio was appalled at the sight.

The Bay St. Louis bridge—a formidable, four-lane concrete structure—had been razed and "stacked like dominoes that had fallen over." Huge piles of wood and other debris littered the Gulf side of Beach Boulevard, and several businesses that had been located on that side of the roadway were completely gone. Down the street, he noticed that a concrete and wood pier, the property of St. Stanislaus Catholic school, also was gone. People were wandering around in shock and disbelief, trying to help each other. Maggio made a mental note: "The thin veneer of civilization that we talk about has held pretty good. People are genuinely interested in each other and not in materialism." Continuing down the beach to Waveland, the doctor found the wreckage of his Whispering Pines Drive home, a 100-year-old dwelling that had just been remodeled. He was shocked to find that the entire lot, except for two large oak trees, had been swept clean. Even the oaks, perched 15 feet above sea level, appeared to be hanging on for dear life. "Everything was going along wonderful," he would say later, "until this grand and glorious, monstrous storm came roaring out of the Gulf one day and ate my house."

Dawn did not bring relief for the crippled Edith de Vries, eastward across the bay in Pass Christian. Lying in debris and unable to walk, but with her eyeglasses firmly in place, she looked around and found she was surrounded by furniture, appliances, and personal objects from her demolished home: a pink refrigerator, a dressing table, one of her husband's French picture frames, and other items. She tried to use a board to balance herself, but fell back into the muck. She spent the day crying out for help and watching airplanes fly overhead, but no rescuers came. Sunburned and nursing a sprained wrist as daylight faded, she was forced to spend another night in the "black bayou mud"—fighting hunger, thirst, rain, the cold, and mosquitos. She was first reported as missing and then dead. It was Tuesday afternoon before Navy Seabees found Mrs. de Vries "dirty, bruised and bloody," and with a blood pressure reading of 90 over 54—but alive. Her daughter, Earle, the Lafollettes, and the three other renters also had survived the storm, battered but alive.

Piet and Valena Stegenga held onto each other and to their plywood umbrella as they weathered the elements on their pile of trash. They could see and hear men with flashlights during the night but received no help. Soaking wet and freezing, all Valena could think about was how much she wanted a cigarette. At daybreak, they looked around and realized they weren't as far from home as they thought. The post office was gone, Ringer's Grocery was gone, and the bank was gone. Piet had lost most of his clothing, his shoes, and eyeglasses. Valena's dress was shredded. She had lost her shoes, even her panties. Both Stegengas were punched full of holes from nails and sore from the pounding of other jagged debris. Valena was about to pass out when Piet spotted a woman standing in the doorway of a nearby, water-gutted house. He recognized her as a neighbor who lived only about 200 feet from their home. Thirsty, they got up and walked over to see if they could get something to drink. "All I can give y'all is a highball. I can't make coffee or anything," said the neighbor, Mrs. Cook. But Valena still wanted that smoke. "Mrs. Cook, do you have a cigarette?" she asked. Mrs. Cook took them into her house and gave them a drink of whiskey, which helped take away the chill. Then, she gave Valena a cigarette and a robe to replace the torn dress. Valena took a long hard drag, savoring the familiar taste. "This is the best cigarette I've ever smoked," she thought.

The Stegengas then walked toward their house, which was located behind Pass Christian High School. They found Joey Dambrink alive, hanging onto the limb of a tree. Their house and yard were a mess, with only the foundation and a portion of the top half of the structure remaining. The backyard contained debris from the ruins of nearby Trinity Episcopal Church. The Dambrink house, located about a block away, was gone too. So too were Pops, Mother, and Sis Dambrink. Piet, Valena, and Joey didn't have to say a word. They knew it. It would be nearly a week after the hurricane before the Dambrinks' bodies would be found. Valena's tears came later. Losing Pops, to her, was like losing a child. He was "feeble-minded." But she understood him. She loved him.

Perched in separate trees in Live Oaks Cemetery, Paul Williams, his son Malcolm, and his son-in-law Nick yelled for help in rotation all through the night; they had no candles to light and were too weary to curse the darkness. Finally, rescuers came with flashlights and pulled them to safety. They rescued the Reverend Durrie Hardin too, although the rectory was gone and his 66-year-old wife, Helen, had died in the storm. Williams looked around at daylight and thought it odd that the storm had lifted the Hardins' car out of the garage and deposited it near Pass Christian High School northeast of the church, with no broken glass and hardly a dent. But nearly all of Williams's family—his wife, 11 of his children, and one grandchild—had perished. Malcolm didn't want his dad to see his mother's body. "Daddy, Mama got her neck broken," he said. Williams complied, at first. Then, later that morning, he helped workers from Riemann Funeral Home recover the bodies, one by one, and place them on a walkway. He insisted that all of the bodies be kept together. Only one was missing. Nearby, Gerald Peralta watched the scene with a heavy heart. "The thing that hurt me the most," he would recall, "was watching that man carrying out the bodies of his family and laying them right there on the sidewalk." Williams just stared as the undertakers put the bodies on ice. "We've got to go on living," he mumbled to himself. "You can't run away from it."

Around 5 a.m., Ben Duckworth saw lights about 30 feet below the sprawling oak tree limb to which he was still clinging with a determined grip. He thought he was hallucinating at first, then realized it was the lights of a search party. Exhausted, he let go of the limb and slid part of the way down the tree before falling into the arms of a brawny rescue worker. Cuts and scratches covered his body, but he was alive. Many others were not. He was taken to Pass Christian High School for treatment. Later, however, and still in shock, he crawled out a window and walked back to the Richelieu, where he found a distraught Rick Keller. "She's gone, she's gone," was all Rick said. Luane was gone. So were Jack and Zoe Matthews, Fritz Gerlach, Shirley Ann Geshke, and at least three others who had been in the apartment complex that fateful night.

Mary Ann Gerlach could hear people shouting as she awoke that morning and could see people walking on the nearby railroad tracks. She yelled for help. A local physician, searching for his wife, walked over to her. "Have you seen Shirley?" he asked, apparently in a state of shock. "Help me," pleaded Mary Ann. But the doctor just turned around "like a zombie" and waded back to the railroad tracks, still looking for Shirley. Mary Ann finally was rescued about 9 a.m. by a local postal worker and a large man, who picked her up in his arms like a baby and carried her to a nearby station wagon. She was treated first at the high school, then transported to Miramar Nursing Home, where a physician sewed up her bleeding knee without the benefit of water or alcohol. Later, she was taken to the base hospital at Keesler, where her knee became infected and "swelled up . . . to the size of one of those icebox water mellons." Two operations and six weeks later, she was released to the care of physical therapists. It was eight days after the storm before they found Fritz's body, dark and swollen from the exposure, resting in the limbs of a tree with a mattress on top of him. Still nearly fully clothed, he was wearing the diamond ring Mary Ann had given him in anticipated celebration of their second wedding anniversary. Fritz was buried near his parents' home in Danforth, Connecticut. Mary Ann went on with her life.

Chief Peralta was shocked that Monday morning to find that the Richelieu had disappeared. He and his crew aboard the LARC had rescued "75 to 80 people" from possible death and certain injury during the night. Now, he looked up and saw a house sitting in the middle of the railroad tracks, where it had been deposited as the tide went out. A train was approaching and a man was out there, desperately trying to flag it down. The town reminded the chief of bombed-out villages he had seen in Vietnam. Masked rescue workers combed the debris for bodies. A young girl who had lost her mother in the storm wandered down the street in a daze, shouting, "Mama." The scene was surreal.

Everywhere, there was the obnoxious whine of chain saws—a sound that would be forever associated with Camille's aftermath in the minds and memories of those who survived.

Pass Christian resident Richard B. Merritt rode out the storm on the roof of his house with his son, Jonathan, young friend Randy Cohen, a poodle, and a little red miniature dachshund named Heidi. Earlier, the 47-year-old former Coast Guard aviator and local real estate developer had evacuated his wife and daughters 70 miles north to Hattiesburg. Now, he wished he had gone too. Heidi's little face had turned completely white during the night.

TRACKING
THE MONSTER

Camille was the most powerful storm to strike the U.S. mainland in modern history and remains today the benchmark by which all other American hurricanes are measured. Only Hurricane Andrew, a Category 5 storm that cut a swath across heavily populated south Florida in 1992, created more destruction. Other storms have matched Camille's strength (Gilbert in 1988, Allen in 1980, and Janet in 1955), but only Camille hit landfall at peak Category 5 intensity. Thanks to the tireless research efforts of Julia Guice and others over the ensuing years, the Mississippi Gulf Coast death toll was finally confirmed at 172—including an actual body count of 131 and another 41 missing and never found. "What we tried to do was put a name with the numbers for all three coastal counties," Guice said in a 2003 interview. Nearly 9,000 more were injured. The damage in today's dollars totaled an estimated $11 billion.

The destruction along the Mississippi Gulf Coast from Ansley to Biloxi was incredible, as antebellum homes, restaurants, motels, apartments, schools, churches, and other structures were swept off their foundations and deposited in mountains of rubble together with trees and automobiles. The atomic-bomb effect of Camille's 200-mile-per-hour wind gusts and 25-foot storm surge destroyed 100 years of growth and progress along the Mississippi Coast in just three hours. Ancient oak trees were uprooted and washed into the mix with piers, signs, vehicles, boats, power poles, roofs, floors, walls, furniture, appliances, and the other scattered residue of civilization. A variety of vessels, including large barges, were lifted from the Gulf and deposited on the beach as sand washed over the seawall, covering or crumbling large portions of U.S. Highway 90. Army engineers and other workers would have to clear away 100,000 tons of debris along some 530 miles of roadway. Bridges spanning St. Louis Bay and Biloxi Bay, including the back-bay bridge at D'Iberville, were knocked out.

Wade and Julia Guice had spent a sleepless night—Wade at the Harrison County Emergency Operations Center in Gulfport and Julia at the civil defense office in Biloxi—not knowing the fate of their home or of their teenaged daughter, Judy. They knew their teenaged sons, Reed and 15-year-old Brent, the youngest of the three children, were safe. With the Gulfport airport runway partially cleared and the wind still gusting strongly, Wade left bright and early that Monday morning to take an aerial survey of the damaged Coast, which included "68 square miles of totally destroyed area" in Harrison County alone. He was astounded at the sight: a mountain of debris piled up along the tide line, as high as 30 feet in some places. Over Pass Christian, he noticed a huge crater in the center of one of the main roads. There was a body floating in it. A woman stumbled through the muck, clutching the lifeless body of a child to her bosom. Only concrete slabs remained where homes and other structures had existed. The 200-ton slabs of the St. Louis Bay bridge had shifted substantially, and the railroad bridge had been stripped clean of its rails. Turning back to the east, Guice was startled to see that the entire eastern tip of Biloxi had been under water. The civil defense director couldn't resist the temptation of looking for his own home, located on Seal Street, just a couple of blocks north of the landmark Biloxi Lighthouse on U.S. Highway 90. He spotted it. There was a huge pile of debris around it and the roof was damaged, but the 66-year-old structure was still intact. Guice breathed a sigh of relief as the light airplane in which he rode headed back to the Gulfport airport and a safe landing. He would spend the next nine days buried in recovery work at the EOC, and, for much of that time, he steadfastly refused to read the death lists accumulated by EOC personnel. It would be five days before he and a frantic Julia heard from their daughter, who was alive and safe.

Based on Red Cross data, Camille's destruction in Mississippi and Louisiana included: 5,662 homes destroyed; 13,915 homes with major damage; 33,933 homes with minor damage; 1,082 mobile homes destroyed; 621 mobile homes with major damage; 775 farm buildings destroyed; 2,289 farm buildings with major damage; 679 small businesses destroyed or with major damage; at least five trucking terminals destroyed; at least 94 vessels sunk or grounded; and 5,000 head of cattle drowned. "In the first week alone, 25 tons of dead animals [including other farm animals, horses, wildlife, and pets] were removed by the military and the Army Corps of Engineers," Biloxi *Sun Herald* newspaper reporter Kat Bergeron wrote in a 1989 story headlined "Camille Was No Lady." Nearly 2 million acres of commercial forests were heavily damaged, railroad tracks were decimated to the tune of $2 million, and 80,000 telephones were silenced. More than 50,000 cars and other vehicles were destroyed or badly damaged.

The damage to Mississippi's seafood industry was unprecedented. Although most Gulf Coast shrimpers rode out the storm and avoided catastrophe by pulling their boats upriver and tying them to trees, it would take a month to clear local fishing waters of mangrove trees and other net-snarling debris. Fortunately, shrimp remained plentiful. Area oyster reefs, however, were hard hit, with the damage estimated at $50,000. The state would spend $1 million to rebuild offshore oyster reefs, and it would cost the federal government another $1 million for reseeding. Some 20 seafood processing plants were damaged or destroyed at a cost of $8 million, an estimated 3,000 to 4,000 people were left unemployed in the storm's wake, and it would take expenditures of $75 million to restore Mississippi's seafood industry.

If hurricanes were rated by size rather than intensity, Camille would rank among the smaller severe storms on record. Its hurricane-force winds extended out only about 45 miles in all directions from the eye as it hit landfall, creating sustained winds of just 44 miles per hour 75 miles east of Bay St. Louis at Mobile and 50-plus-mile-per-hour winds 60 miles west at New Orleans. Gales and tornadoes spawned by the killer storm extended out 150 miles. The three Mississippi Gulf Coast counties—Hancock, Harrison, and Jackson, with their combined population of 240,000—suffered the brunt of the storm's destruction, along with the extreme southeastern portion of Louisiana that included Plaquemines and St. Bernard parishes and the southwest segment of Alabama encompassing Mobile and Baldwin counties, as well as Dauphin Island. Wade Guice would always believe, however, that last-minute mass evacuations prompted by timely reconnaissance flight reports of Camille's 26.84 barometric pressure and 200-plus-mile-per-hour winds proved the "difference between survival and 10,000 tombstones" on the Mississippi Coast that terrible night of hell and heartache.

Fishing vessels, crew boats, and other craft were picked up by the surge of water just east of the mouth of the Mississippi River and lifted atop levees or washed inland as nature's weapon of mass destruction followed a north-

northeasterly path toward the Mississippi beachfront. In Louisiana's Buras Township, a large oil barge was lifted over a levee and deposited on the main highway, barely missing a nearby power plant and transformer complex. Demolition of the low-lying Louisiana bayou country was complete from Venice to north of Ft. Jackson, with only structures of reinforced concrete standing up to Camille's power—but evacuation of the area was nearly 100 percent. East of the river in Breton Sound, offshore oil rigs toppled like dominoes. New Orleans was spared the full force of the hurricane winds, although buildings in eastern portions of the city suffered a great deal of glass and roof damage. Water rose to nearly six and a half feet in New Orleans's Industrial Canal and at Seabrook Bridge, considerable but considerably less than the 10-foot storm surge that had struck the port of New Orleans during Hurricane Betsy four years earlier.

In Alabama, most of the damage occurred on Dauphin Island and northward to the coastal area around Mobile and Prichard, where rising water reached a depth of about seven and a half feet, covering the Alabama state docks but causing negligible damage. No lives were lost. Farther east, at Pensacola, Florida, a shrimp boat and a barge sank in the harbor.

Between 9:30 p.m. and 11 p.m. on the night of August 17, Camille ripped the Mississippi Gulf Coast to shreds. The western eye of the storm passed between Waveland and Clermont Harbor, and the eastern edge passed through Bay St. Louis. Clermont Harbor was leveled, and hundreds of beach homes were swept away eastward in Waveland and Bay St. Louis, where the heavy damage stretched several blocks inland. Farther east across the bay, the water rose to 22 feet in Pass Christian and obliterated Henderson Point except for one enduring structure, a former maritime academy. Oaks were uprooted or stripped of limbs and leaves, and many pine trees were snapped at 10 to 15 feet above the ground. Only a slab and swimming pool filled with trash and seawater remained where the Richelieu Manor apartment complex had stood.

To the east, past equally devastated Long Beach, the busy port of Gulfport was smashed and the beachfront littered with shattered homes and commercial buildings. Three large cargo ships—*Alamo Victory, Silver Hawk,* and *Hulda*—were washed aground on the north end of the harbor. Structures at the banana wharf were stripped of their sheet metal, and cargo from the wharf warehouses was tossed hither and yon, including huge rolls of paper weighing several tons. Tugboats and commercial fishing craft were torn from their moorings, and, like the numerous pleasure boats, now pleasureless, they mingled with the mangled ruins of miscellaneous beachfront properties. Perched on the medial strip between the east and west lanes of U.S. Highway 90 was a large diesel fuel barge that had been scooped out of the harbor like a kid's toy.

Eastward at Biloxi, the beachfront damage also was severe. At first glance, the modern marina fronting the Broadwater Beach Hotel appeared to be relatively unscathed. On closer examination, however, it could be seen that chunks of molded concrete covering the boat slips were broken off and buildings housing shops near the entrance were demolished. The dredge, *Lima*, sank in the harbor, and a number of motor yachts sank in their slips or were carried away. East, across Biloxi Bay, Ocean Springs and Gautier were wrecked by the storm, and beyond that, in Pascagoula, Mississippi's easternmost municipality before the Alabama state line, a large freighter was torn from its moorings at Ingalls Shipyard and deposited on high ground near a port elevator.

As newspaper reporter Steve Brunsman noted in an August 19, 1989, article in the Biloxi *Sun Herald*, Camille paid no respect to religion in her frenzied rush to destroy. Houses of worship were splintered along the length of the Mississippi Coast. St. Ann Catholic Church in Clermont Harbor and Christ Episcopal Church in Bay St. Louis were destroyed, as was St. Louis King of France Church, also located in Hancock County. St. Clare Catholic Church in Waveland was heavily damaged. At Christ Episcopal, the storm surge transported 15-year-old Elizabeth Johnson Benvenutti and other family members right out of the Beach Boulevard house that served as the church rectory. The house, some 16 feet above sea level, was flooded, but the family survived by swimming to a nearby vacant house. "Material things didn't mean as much after Camille," Elizabeth said later.

In Pass Christian, First Methodist Church and St. Paul Catholic Church were demolished, and the Gulfshore

Baptist Assembly buildings on Henderson Point had all but disappeared. The city's 120-year-old Trinity Episcopal Church, where Paul Williams had huddled with his family, was gone, as was the church rectory. In Long Beach, St. Thomas Catholic Church and St. Patrick's Episcopal Church were destroyed, and First Baptist Church was severely damaged. The clergy had fled St. Thomas Catholic Church as Camille approached. When parishioner Joe Van Cloostere, then 73, combed through the remains of the structure the next morning, he uncovered a pair of empty church steps. Later, he recalled, "It looked a battering ram had been working all night. The front was all rubble, and two barges were sitting out front." An American flag was unfurled from the two front steps of the church a week later, on Sunday, August 24, as the Reverend Francis O'Malley, St. Thomas's pastor, celebrated Mass amid the ruins in a service that was broadcast on national radio.

In Gulfport, Camille destroyed St. John Catholic Church, heavily damaged St. Mark's Episcopal Church, and caused bad water damage at First Baptist and First Presbyterian churches. The new pastor at St. Mark's, the Reverend James "Bo" Roberts, then 27, rode out the storm in the attic of the wood-frame Church Avenue rectory with his wife, three children, and mother. The rectory, which was 22 feet above sea level, later would house a kindergarten. The church was pushed off its foundation by the storm and lodged against a lone pine tree, which kept the structure from washing away. The tree, subsequently dubbed "The Tree That Saved St. Mark's," was a landmark until it was destroyed later by Hurricane Elena.

In Biloxi, St. Michael's Catholic Church was gutted, along with its school, and the Episcopal Church of the Redeemer, located just blocks west, was destroyed. Only the historic belltower was left standing at the Church of the Redeemer, which was hit while its rector, the Reverend Jack Biggers, was in Malawi working as part of a church mission. At St. Michael's, two Roman Catholic priests, the Reverend Morgan Kavanaugh and the Reverend George Murphy, rode out the hurricane inside the church. They made themselves comfortable and planned to watch the storm from the church veranda, but shivered when they saw a bowling pin floating down an aisle. Murphy, then 26 and serving his first parish assignment, said, "That's when it hit me. If the bowling pin is now in the church, where might the bowling alley be?" Highly motivated by that time, Kavanaugh grabbed hold of a Virgin Mary statue on a side altar and Murphy locked his arms around a statue of St. Joseph. According to Brunsman, Murphy remembered that "The statues, fastened to steel girters, held fast. The interior of the church was gutted."

A number of Mississippi Coast landmarks also were ravaged by Camille. Pass Christian's Dixie White House—where President Woodrow Wilson spent two and a half weeks recovering from the flu during the Christmas season of 1913—was gutted beyond repair. The house, which had been built in 1854, originally was called Beaulieu. Also destroyed was Waveland's Old Pirate

House, built in 1802 and reputed to have been a getaway refuge for Louisiana pirate Jean Lafitte. The ghosts of murdered pirates were said to have roamed the beachfront dwelling. In neighboring Bay St. Louis, the last of the once-numerous beachfront gazebos disappeared in the storm.

In Biloxi, Beauvoir, the last home of Confederate president Jefferson Davis, was heavily damaged. Trees on the historic grounds, where Davis had written his famous post–Civil War memoirs, were twisted, broken, and scattered. One employee died of a heart attack there during the height of the hurricane, but the antebellum structure survived because of a raised design that protected its main floor from the storm surge. The Davis Family Museum, however, housed at the time in an area underneath the main house, suffered severe damage. Beauvoir was closed for a long period of time in Camille's aftermath, but later was restored with the aid of state appropriations and a private fund-raising campaign that generated donations from across the country.

Friendship Oak—the massive, sprawling oak tree that predates Christopher Columbus's arrival in the New World—survived Camille at the Long Beach site of a former women's college, which has served since 1972 as the Gulf Coast campus of the University of Southern Mississippi. Kat Bergeron, whose careful and exhaustive reporting over the years has provided a wealth of post-Camille data, wrote the following in an August 13, 1989, article headlined "Friendship Oak Helps Replant Coast Trees":

The murderous winds swirling around Hurricane Camille's eye buffeted the Mississippi Coast's oldest resident to no avail. Left leafless, but with life and limbs still intact, the 500-year-old Friendship Oak refused to join thousands of other trees prostrated by the 210 mph winds in 1969. Forever a friend to man, the giant oak on the Long Beach campus of the University of Southern Mississippi became a spouting symbol of hope. Four years after the storm, 100,000 Friendship Oak babies were planted from Waveland to Pascagoula and inland to Wiggins . . . The old Pirate House, the Shoo-fly, the Merry Mansions and other landmarks could not be replanted, but trees could be replanted.

As shocked and shattered survivors prayed in darkness, clinging to the rubble and ruin of what had been their homes and businesses that August night, Camille moved inland with its deadly fury still in tow. From Biloxi's once-proud and now-splintered Buena Vista Hotel to the scenic town of Buena Vista, Virginia, located in the eastern shadows of the Blue Ridge Mountains, the storm would carve a yet-unimaginable path of death and destruction before playing out its hand of aces and eights in the Atlantic Ocean some five days later.

As Camille moved overland across Mississippi on August 18, it ripped through pastures, forests, and towns along its path with winds that caused moderate damage some 35 miles inland at Wiggins in Stone County. Poplarville and surrounding Pearl River County suffered more than $35 million in damage. More than 35,000 acres of tung trees and 10 million pounds of pecans were lost in the storm, and 85 percent of the area's dairy farms were damaged or destroyed. Much of the damage was attributed to tornadoes spawned by Camille. Heavy rains of 6–10 inches accompanying the storm drenched south Mississippi—including 10.6 inches recorded in a 16-hour period some 70 miles inland at Hattiesburg in Forrest County—and sparked minor flash flooding throughout low-lying areas. For several days after the hurricane, Army helicopter crews would busy themselves rescuing pockets of storm survivors marooned by floodwaters north of Bay St. Louis, west of Wiggins, and south of Poplarville. Eventually, some 33 Mississippi counties would qualify for some kind of federal disaster assistance stemming from the hurricane.

For the most part, however, damage beyond Wiggins was restricted to tree-limb losses and power failures. Jackson, located 160 miles inland, recorded a barometric pressure of 28.93 inches and wind gusts of up to 67 miles an hour, as Camille's eye passed east of the capital city about 8 a.m. on the 18th. An identifiable storm circulation also extended into Quitman County in east-central Mississippi. Paul Ussery, state director of Emergency Welfare Services at the time, remembered that "the wind was blowing so hard, the red lights were horizontal" at the downtown Jackson intersection of State and Capitol streets. Later, as he drove south to help organize the distribution of food and supplies to Gulf Coast victims, he recalled an "eerie feeling. When I got just south of Hattiesburg, there wasn't a light anywhere. It was total darkness."

The hurricane weakened as it moved into north Mississippi and was downgraded to tropical depression status, with sustainable winds of less than 39 miles per hour by the time it reached the state's northern border with Tennessee. Camille's appetite for death and destruction had not been diminished, however, as remnants of the storm moved on a northeasterly course across Tennessee, Kentucky, and Ohio before veering into West Virginia and southern Virginia. Two inches of rainfall actually relieved drought conditions in portions of Tennessee and Kentucky. But the misleading lull ended about 7 p.m. Tuesday, August 19, as storm-driven torrential rains began pounding the eastern slopes of the Blue Ridge Mountains in a record deluge that was to continue for eight hours. Most residents of Virginia's James River basin—a 100-mile long, 50-mile-wide corridor from Clifton Forge to Richmond, and from Waynesboro to Fredericksburg—turned in for the night, unaware of the wall of water that soon would be descending upon them. In his October 1969 article "The James River Flood of August 1969 in Virginia," Herbert J. Thompson wrote:

> *A combination of metereological factors produced torrential rains, which rank with other record rainfalls throughout the world. Surveys found one confirmed amount of thirty-one inches and several of more than twenty-five inches. Rainfall in excess of four inches fell over an area thirty to 40 miles*

wide and one hundred and twenty miles long, most of it
occurring in a period of eight hours . . . Most of the residents
of the mountain hollows, hamlets and towns were asleep
when the storm began. Little warning was possible . . .
Rapidly rising streams and landslides caused by the
unprecedented rainfall not only destroyed homes as the
occupants slept, but tore out communication lines and
roads, preventing downstream inhabitants from being
alerted . . . This storm was one of nature's rare events . . .
Rainfall of this magnitude occurs, on the average, only once
in more than one-thousand years.

More than 10 inches of rainfall inundated Clifton
Forge and the eastern mountain range slopes, turning
uprooted trees into battering rams, smashing through
houses, and overturning automobiles as the water moved
downstream. The towns of Buena Vista and Covington,
alerted by the rapid rise in river stages, managed to evacuate residents, with only one loss of life. Crest stages at
Palmyra on the Rivanna River and Buena Vista on the
Maury River exceeded previous record flood stages dating to 1936 by 10 and eight and a half feet, respectively.
The Maury dumped five and a half feet of water into
Buena Vista's downtown business district, and floodwaters almost 14 feet virtually destroyed the business district
of Glasgow, located at the confluence of the Maury and
James rivers. Downtown Waynesboro was engulfed by
floodwaters eight feet deep from the South River. The Tye
and Rockfish river watersheds in Nelson County, how-

ever, were hardest hit by the flooding. The disaster areas also included Albermarle, Amherst, Fluvanna, Rockbridge, Alleghany, Bath, Botetourt, Buckingham, Cumberland, Goochland, Orange, and Powhatan counties.

Most of the river towns along the James River from Lynchburg to Richmond were wrecked. Crest stages exceeded those of the 1936 flood at all points on the river below Buchanan—including Bremo Bluff, Columbia, Holcombs Rock, and Cartersville—and were exceeded only by floodmarks dating to the 1870s at Lynchburg, Scottsville, and the city locks of Richmond. "Richmond, with 36 hours warning, was well prepared for the flood crest. Low-lying areas of the city were flooded when a sewage pumping plant had to be closed due to threatened structural damage and floodwaters backed up through sewer lines," wrote Thompson.

Camille's refusal to die quietly turned into Virginia's worst-ever natural disaster. In the wake of the flooding and landslides, the storm left 106 dead, 67 missing, and 102 injured. Two people lost their lives in West Virginia. The property damage exceeded $100 million. Virginia's Nelson County suffered the most. Of the 162 dead and missing, 126 were residents of Nelson County—"a little more than one percent of the county's population." Of 313 homes destroyed by Camille, 250 were located in the county, as were 225 of 415 houses suffering major damage. The flash flooding knocked out all but one north-south highway traversing the state. Some 133 bridges were destroyed or damaged, and 25 miles of primary and 175 miles of secondary roads were demolished, with a damage estimate totaling $19 million.

By Wednesday afternoon, August 20, Camille had exited Virginia over Chesapeake Bay east of Norfolk and regained tropical intensity off the Atlantic Coast. By Friday, August 22, however, the freak of nature lost its identity as a tropical storm when it merged with a frontal system about 175 miles southeast of Cape Race, Newfoundland. Quietly, it drifted out to sea and died—leaving more than 250 dead, billions of dollars in damages, and incalculable human suffering and heartache in its wake.

Back on the Mississippi Gulf Coast, there was no food, water, ice, or fuel; roads, bridges, airports, and railways had been rendered useless; 15,000 people were homeless; and thousands dug their way out of the wreckage, many wandering zombie-like through the shattered landscape. Patients and residents of area hospitals and nursing homes, including some 800 patients at the Gulfport hospital, were evacuated to medical facilities in Jackson and other inland points by Air National Guard planes from Keesler Air Force Base. Navy Seabees based in Gulfport searched for survivors, helped with evacuation missions, and assisted in the cleanup operations, as did airmen from Keesler.

President Richard Nixon declared south Mississippi, as well as portions of western Alabama and eastern Louisiana, to be federal disaster areas, ordering nearly 1,500 U.S. 3rd Army soldiers and about 800 Army engineers to the area to help maintain order and clear away debris. They brought tons of food, vehicles, and aircraft with them. The president also sent Vice President Spiro Agnew to the Coast as his personal representative. Mississippi governor John Bell Williams, who had lost an arm in a World War II plane crash, declared martial law and established a 6 p.m. to 6 a.m. curfew. The state highway patrol, assisted by military police, sealed off all roads leading into and out of the storm-stricken area to prevent the immediate return of refugees who had fled north and others who might exacerbate the chaotic conditions. Williams also opened Camp Shelby, the sprawling National Guard training site just south of Hattiesburg, dormitories of the University of Southern Mississippi, and Jackson's Robert E. Lee Hotel for survivors who had lost their homes.

At the Harrison County EOC, workers added little red fingers to a Gulf Coast map each day to indicate areas in which electrical power had been restored, which meant water pumps also could function again. "The little fingers of life reached out a little bit farther into the community," Wade Guice remembered. The Gulfport airport was utilized as a centralized area for receiving and distributing water to neighborhood centers and churches, with Borden Milk and the Jax Brewery Company suspending their normal area operations in order to furnish much of the containerized water badly needed by Gulf Coast residents. Guice recalled only scattered incidents of hoarding, price-fixing, and looting in the immediate aftermath of Camille, but noted that "rich and poor alike literally stood in line for their daily ration, for many days . . ." National Guard commanders deployed soldiers all along the Coast, however, with orders to take all necessary measures to prevent looting. A firefight was reported in Ocean Springs when National Guardsmen were fired upon by armed looters and returned the fire, but no casualties were reported as the looters fled.

On top of all this, there was a growing vermin control problem. Insects "flourished in the intense August heat, feeding on rotting animal carcasses and debris left by the storm, while rodents sifted through garbage and spoiled food." What could not be safely burned—primarily because of broken gas mains and a shortage of water—was buried. Army engineers buried the putrid remains of thousands of domestic animals, wild animals, and house-hold pets at 27 disposal sites—some 25 tons of cows, horses, deer, raccoons, opossums, birds, dogs, cats, and snakes that had died in the storm surge. The hurricane was particularly hard on pets. Historian Charles Sullivan wrote, "One German Shepherd, hurled into the Gulfport Public Library by the storm, was found crushed to death under a fallen book rack in the children's section. The shelf under which the dog lay bore the legend: 'Animals We Love.' Many pets not killed by the storm had to be destroyed because no facilities or food existed for their care. Regular Army troops, many of them veterans of Vietnam, reportedly wept as they shot them down." Early on the 18th, four low-flying aircraft from Keesler began spraying malathion to an area 54 miles long and nine miles deep to attack insects and other vermin, and dropped 100,000 pounds of Mirex through the area in an effort to control fire ants, which had survived by tumbling through the waves in balls.

The U.S. Army provided a specially trained scout dog platoon to help lead searchers to the bodies of Camille victims, and four Army mortuary teams also assisted with the grisly task of identification. It would be a month, however, before the final body was recovered. As Wade Guice remembered: "We found the body of the last Camille victim on the 31st day under a mountain of debris, four and a half blocks from where his home had been destroyed. That was the hurricane-proof house, same as always."

The governor lifted martial law at midnight on August 27, although a military presence continued for some time. On September 8, some three weeks after the storm, President and Mrs. Nixon flew into the Biloxi-Gulfport Regional Airport aboard *Air Force One*. They were greeted by thousands of flag-waving Mississippians, national media coverage, and a military band that played "Dixie" along with a variety of other patriotic airs. In remarks to the enthusiastic throng, Nixon expressed confidence that the Gulf Coast would overcome its adversity and rebuild.

Insurance companies would pay out more than $200 million in claims during the ensuing weeks and months, but that would cover only about 20 percent of the actual hurricane damage. Because most Gulf Coast residents had little or no flood insurance protection, many claims became ensnarled in debate over whether the cause of damage was wind or water. Comedian Bob Hope flew to the state and conducted a "We Care" telethon at the Mississippi Coliseum in Jackson—an event that sparked an outpouring of gifts and other aid to the Gulf Coast, ranging from the nickels and dimes of schoolchildren to a gift of $100,000 from the business community in St. Petersburg, Florida.

The August 19 federal disaster declaration paved the way for government assistance to thousands of displaced storm survivors whose homes had been wiped out or heavily damaged. A variety of federal and state agencies, military units, churches, and volunteer relief organizations such as the American Red Cross and the Salvation Army pitched in to begin providing food, shelter, clothing, and medical supplies. The Office of Emergency Preparedness (OEP) took over coordination of the massive relief effort by at least 25 agencies and organizations. The federal Department of Housing and Urban Development (HUD) contributed 5,000 mobile homes, some 3,000 of which were used in Mississippi. Victims began moving in only a week after Camille hit. The U.S. Department of Defense provided 16,500 military personnel from different service branches. The Army brought in food, medicine, and potable water and assisted with helicopter rescue efforts to remove storm survivors from remote locations. The U.S. Army Corps of Engineers cleared roadways and removed more than 37 tons of debris. The U.S. Department of the Treasury established hurricane emergency offices that, by December 10, 1969, had disbursed 75,000 checks totaling $25 million in the form of rehabilitation loans. The Department of Justice's Community Relations Service (CRS) acquired, stored, and distributed up to 50 tons of bedding that had weathered the storm intact at the Hotel Biloxi, and passed along 40,000 textbooks donated by New York school districts. The Federal Bureau of Investigation (FBI) also helped coroners process some 30 unidentified hurricane victims.

The U.S. Department of Agriculture helped attack the pest problem by supplying pesticides to quell the increase in insects that were making life miserable for survivors and rescue workers alike. The agency provided more than $2.5 million in emergency conservation funds to rehabilitate farmlands and conservation structures damaged by Camille. As of November 28, 1969, the Farmers Home Administration (FHA) had okayed 353 emergency loans totaling $3 million for Mississippi farmers. Another federal agency, the Department of Commerce, weighed in with help for damaged communities through its Economic Development Administration (EDA). The agency identified 28 public works and business loan projects totaling $30 million (in 1969 dollars) as eligible for EDA assistance, and provided economic planning and development support to deal with the sudden rise in unemployment. Also, the Weather Bureau joined with the

Defense Department in a study aimed at improving ways to predict the direction and intensity of hurricanes.

The U.S. Department of Health provided more than $4 million in materials, services, and funds to the storm-ravaged area—including cots, blankets, typhoid vaccines, and other medical supplies. The department also brought in temporary classrooms to assist 21 local school districts that had received damage. The Food and Drug Administration (FDA) surveyed area food establishments to make sure safety and health code requirements were enforced. The American Red Cross had set up shelters to accommodate up to 85,000 persons before the storm, and Red Cross volunteers manned relief centers after the storm, disbursing services, food stamps, and other forms of assistance. Altogether, the Red Cross assigned 913 volunteers and 805 professional staff to the affected area. The relief work of the Salvation Army was extensive, as countless storm survivors would later attest, but the organization's contributions were impossible to calculate.

The National Aeronautics and Space Administration's Mississippi Test Facility (renamed the Stennis Space Center in 1988) in Hancock County, still basking in the success of the July moon landing, turned its attention away from rocket testing for the next few months after Camille to help the Coast rebound. Having suffered less than $1 million in damages—mostly from scattered roofing materials—the facility became a refugee center for some 7,000 storm victims.

The final tab in aid and other forms of assistance to the Mississippi Coast in Camille's aftermath was estimated years later at $488 million. That included $214.6 million in insurance company settlements; $120 million in Small Business Administration (SBA) low-interest loans; $54.3 million from the U.S. Army Corps of Engineers; $30 million from the Economic Development Administration; $15 million from the Department of Housing and Urban Development; $10 million-plus from the Red Cross; $10 million in grants and loans from the state of Mississippi; $8 million for road and bridge repairs; $6,260,470 from the Farmers Home Administration; $4,415,401 from the U.S. Department of Agriculture; $4,223,553 from the Interim Home Assistance Program; $4,173,856 in unemployment compensation; $2,029,616 from the Interim Town Assistance Program; $1 million from Bob Hope's "We Care" fund; and $960,000 from the U.S. 3rd Army.

Jerry DeLaughter, in a 1979 article for *The South Magazine* entitled "Ten Years After Camille," wrote: "To Coast residents, real heroes of the immediate recovery were the American Red Cross, the tireless National Guard, Navy Seabees and airmen from Keesler [Air Force Base], selfless volunteers from the Salvation Army, the Seventh-Day Adventist and Mennonite-Amish churches, and countless others who cared." D. L. "Chick" Anderson, manager of the Mississippi Research and Development Center's Gulf Coast field office, also noted: "The hurricane pulled people together and got them moving."

A few days after the storm, Lucille Moody of Gulfport decided to inspect her beachfront lot. Resting on a pile of debris on the otherwise vacant property was a tugboat named *East Point.* The 72-foot boat, later called the SS *Hurricane Camille,* had been washed ashore as the storm surge rose to about 15 feet above Moody's lot. She bought the tug from its local owner, had railroad tracks laid down, and moved the vessel some 200 feet to its current location. Within a year, Moody would transform the grounded tug into a unique tourist attraction called the Camille Gift Shop.

THE SURVIVORS

Dawn along the Mississippi Gulf Coast on the morning of August 18, 1969, was accompanied by a clear sky, billowing white clouds, blustery winds, and subsiding sea. The sunrise also revealed horrors beyond description. Airman Gregory Durrschmidt, surveying the carnage east and west from his station at Keesler Air Force Base, thought, "The Gulf Coast looks like a war zone. Destruction fits one of two categories—demolished or gone." Sand and a few scattered cinder blocks were all that remained of the Biloxi strip's once-festive Fiesta Club. Baricev's Restaurant—where Durrschmidt and his buddies had dined just two nights earlier—was gone except for a couple of concrete walls and a sign. Looking far out into the Gulf, he could see the outline of Ship Island, which had been cut in half by Camille, and the dark silhouette of old Fort Massachusetts, battered but intact. Not much time to reflect. Durrschmidt and his fellow soldiers began searching the coastal wreckage for survivors, finding instead only the bodies of victims, some "faceless and dismembered. Everywhere the smell of rotting flesh fills the hot, humid air." Hundreds of homes were now only unrecognizable piles of debris. "What has happened to my beloved Biloxi, my tropical paradise?" wondered Durrschmidt. The answer was easy. It was gone with the wind—and water.

In Pass Christian, Gerald Peralta and others searched the ruins for the living and the dead, the scene before him evoking memories of the bombed-out hamlets he had seen in Vietnam. The police chief had already exchanged his water-soaked uniform and shoes for cutoff shorts, T-shirt, and sneakers. Dangling from a belt around Peralta's waist was a holster containing his .38-caliber revolver. He was still on duty.

On St. Louis Avenue, right behind the Richelieu complex, 66-year-old Fred DeMetz, his wife, Lillian, his daughter Dorothy Mae DeMetz Niolet, and seven other family members had ridden out the storm terrified but safe in the attic of their home, which had been engulfed by seven feet of water and battered by debris from the disintegrating Richelieu. "I had the impression we were in a boat out in rough water . . . My biggest thought was [that] we had floated out into the Gulf," Niolet remembered. Fred DeMetz, a carpenter and lifelong resident of the city, was sure their lives had been spared only through divine intervention. "I'm not a religious man," he said, but, "the Lord was there and the reason I know he was there is because we prayed to him and he answered our prayers . . . The Lord was helping us, knowing that we were in the attic. It was the only house that wasn't torn up." Fred's sister-in-law was not so lucky. Bonnie DeMetz, the 78-year-old wife of Fred's brother, Charles, drowned when the couple's beachfront home was swept away. Her body was recovered later from the wreckage.

As Peralta worked his way eastward toward Pass Christian High School, the sun was shining brightly. He walked past the ruins of Trinity Episcopal Church, where he saw Paul Williams picking up the bodies of his dead family members. "If we'd stayed home, we might have been safe—all of us," the caretaker muttered to himself, as if he were somehow to blame for the tragedy. Meanwhile, the Reverend Durrie Hardin, whose wife Helen, 66, had died in the collapse of the church rectory, braced himself against the pain of his own personal sorrow by comforting others who had survived. As debris was cleared from a demolished house, Peralta saw the bodies of a woman and child lying in a bed, as if asleep. "The bed was sitting there and she was in the bed with the little girl in her arms . . . She had the kid up against her and her face was turned sideways." Meanwhile, Richard Merritt emerged from his waterlogged home with his white-faced dog, Heidi, and took stock of the damage all around him. Walking through the neighborhood, he came upon a neighbor whose wife had drowned in the storm surge. "He was standing in his yard in his underwear and really seemed to be in terrible shock . . . He didn't recognize me," Merritt remembered.

John Switzer had a sick feeling in his stomach when he arrived for an inspection of his two-year-old Ocean Springs home, which had taken five feet of water and was a shambles. Bricks were scattered along the southern and western walls of the house, and on the south side "there was a hole all the way through the wall that you could walk through." Sewers had backed up through commodes and bathtubs, adding more sludge to the already horrible mess. Most everything was gone, from lawnmower to shoes, yet the family crystal was unbroken. A coffee table had floated upright through the storm, with little Jimmy Switzer's glass of unspilled Coca-Cola resting on top.

The weather was hot and muggy, but it was dead quiet. The trees had been stripped of their leaves and limbs, and there wasn't a bird to be seen or heard. Switzer saw a snake and quickly killed it. Then, he heard the sound of yells coming from the home of his next-door neighbor, Andy Anderson. Switzer rushed over, kicked open a door and discovered Anderson and his wife and two children still hiding in the attic. He took them down to the bank for safekeeping, noting they were in pretty rough shape from the ordeal.

By now, there were looters in Switzer's Ocean Springs neighborhood, some of them arriving in boats to plunder and steal. Exactly where they came from, nobody seemed to know for sure. But they came. Said Switzer, "You see that kind of thing, and it just makes you want to kill." After a load of plywood was stolen from his damaged property, the banker maintained an overnight vigil in his ruined house with a gun as his only companion. "I bought a .38, strapped it on, wore it from dark till the next morning . . . I would have killed anybody that came in there."

Only the doorsteps of Alma Anderson's Biloxi home were left intact. Alma, her husband, her mother-in-law, Uncle Roy, and the two children were beat up but alive. The two elderly aunts were dead, their bodies out there somewhere in the debris. The survivors had been stripped of most of their clothing, even their shoes—yet Alma could not bring herself to cry. No tears. She felt only numbness, remembering, "In winds that strong and with the water, you're like a matchstick: any way it takes you, you are going . . . I don't think, really, that people realize just how precious life is until they come that close to going." Someone had given Alma a size 40 dress and now she fastened it into place around her scratched and bruised frame with safety pins. There was no water for washing or bathing, and there would be no sleep for Alma until the missing family members were located days later.

At Biloxi's Broadwater Beach Hotel, it would be nearly two weeks before Charles Webb's missing, blue-eyed Siamese cat was found in a back room of the pro shop, still frightened but alive. "He was kind of nuts anyway," Webb said of the cat, which lived to the ripe old age of 19. All of the Webbs' personal possessions—including two cars and a mahogany dining room set—were gone or damaged beyond repair. The hotel and golf course fared no better. Brick walls were demolished and the service drive was no longer distinguishable. Stoves, sinks, and an ice maker were cleaned out of the clubhouse. Golf balls, shoes, and clubs were strewn all over the place—as were 80 golf carts, pieces of the roof from the pro shop and golf cart shed, and the limbs of some 1,500 damaged or destroyed trees that had shaded the course. "What a jack-ass I had been," Webb thought. "Why didn't I leave?"

Robert Taylor's beautiful Gulfport neighborhood was demolished. His own home had been gutted, as had most other dwellings that were still standing. Taylor was relieved to find that a couple of neighbors who lived across the street, Vince and Nathan Alfonso, also had survived. He couldn't help chuckling to himself, however, as the two brothers embarked on a frantic search-and-rescue mission for Nathan's missing false teeth. The search provided a bit of comic relief in the midst of disaster, but the laughter would be short-lived.

After walking with Billy and Mary Evelyn to Barrett's Second Street home, the trio heard shots. Taylor hurriedly proceeded alone to check on his mother's nearby home, which also was gutted but standing. A house on one side was completely gone and a two-story house on the other side was now a one-story house. What he saw in his mother's yard stunned him. There were two women picking up silver and other valuables, and stuffing the loot into a big gunnysack. He recalled, "It's the only time in my life I've ever struck a woman . . . I slapped the lady with the sack and took the sack and walked to Mother's home . . . threw the sack up on the second floor [the staircase was gone] and walked out." Just west of his mother's house was the home of a retired University of Southern Mississippi professor and his wife, the Elkemers, and Taylor thought he'd check on the aging couple. Prying open a window with a board, he found them still dressed in their nightclothes, distressed but in good physical condition. "First, they handed me their dog," he said.

Still worried about looters, Taylor briskly covered the two blocks back to his own house and found that his concern was warranted. Four young men were in his front yard picking up silverware, racing trophies, anything shiny. Quickly but quietly, Taylor walked into his home, found a shotgun and some shells, and went back outside. He recalled, "I walked into the yard and told them to put things down, that I didn't want to shoot anyone, but that I'd had enough—and just to leave. All but one left. One just glared at me . . . I threw a shell in the chamber. At that, he turned and flung down the piece of silver . . . said he'd be back and left."

Army National Guardsmen plucked Lois Toomer, her crippled sister, and Mary Fitzpatrick from the sister's storm-shattered house in Long Beach and took them northward to the nearby ruins of a garden club. Local firefighters provided coffee and blankets, and the exhausted women fell onto the ground. Lois hoped her husband would come for them, but it would be days before she would see him. Her sister's husband was in a Mobile, Alabama, hospital at the time. Finally, the women gathered their strength and walked to a nearby bank, dodging fallen power lines and other obstacles as they went. Amazingly, the local bank where they maintained accounts was intact and open for business, and they cashed their checks.

Later, when Lois returned to her east beach home in Gulfport, she found that everything—even her marble-top furniture—had been swept out by the storm surge. Doors and windows of the brick structure were smashed, and debris filled the yard. Scattered along the driveway was Mrs. Toomer's silverware, which she thought she had safely packed away. She recalled, "I didn't even bend to pick it up because that wasn't important." In back of the main house was a little cottage, built in 1906 and adored by Lois. The cottage and its contents, and a widower who rented the dwelling from the Toomers, had ridden out the hurricane in relatively good shape. At the height of the storm, however, the renter had been shocked to look out a window and see his car floating by. "He ran and caught the end of it and pulled it back," Lois later explained.

Seventy-three-year-old Edith de Vries, nursing a cracked wrist and other minor injuries inflicted by Camille, was rescued from the carnage in Pass Christian by Navy Seabees and transported by ambulance to Gulf-port Memorial Hospital. From there, she was taken to Keesler Air Force Base medical facilities and then was flown to Jackson, where she was hospitalized along with her daughter, Earle, who was nursing a foot injury. Edith's husband had survived in the Gulfport nursing home. Meanwhile, Edith learned that the news of her own death had been greatly exaggerated. "I was first reported missing, then dead," she recalled. Upon returning to Pass Christian on September 2, Edith and Earle found that the water had risen to a height of seven feet in their home, and had deposited mud as high as a doorway. Just about everything was gone. "The front steps were all that were left of our home," said Edith. Nevertheless, she remained undaunted by the tragedy. "We go from here," she told Earle.

The hospital in Bay St. Louis, which had been virtually cut off on all sides by the rising storm waters, was evacuated and closed down. About 50 patients were taken out by helicopter. Dr. Henry Maggio had spent the night at the hospital and did not personally witness looting, although he said there were reports that some looters were on the scene as early as 4 o'clock that morning. Local law enforcement officers, however, backed by National Guardsmen, moved in quickly to maintain order. Maggio remembered a degree of emotional, rather than physiological, shock among survivors: "There were people walking around in dazed disbelief—knowing, yet trying to deny and trying to reconcile, that they had just been through something historical."

After surveying the wreckage of his own home on Waveland's Whispering Pines Drive, the doctor and a friend, Charlie Johnson, drove to New Orleans, while Maggio's wife and children headed to north Mississippi and his wife's family home in Batesville. After a few days in the Big Easy, Maggio returned to the Mississippi Coast, obtained a cot from the National Guard, and moved into his Bay St. Louis office, which miraculously had escaped serious damage. Generators were brought in to get the hospital operational again, and Maggio went back to work.

Father Kennedy, a young Irish priest stationed at St. Clare's Catholic Church in Waveland, was everywhere at once after the storm, helping those he could and administering last rites to those he could not. "He gave a moral boost and helped a lot of people," said Alderman Johnny Longo. "The fact you could see a person of God . . . in and out of the debris through the hurricane area, administering to the people, to their moral and mental welfare, was a fine sight." Sister Ruth assisted the priest, and Dr. Marion Dodson, Maggio's medical colleague, worked tirelessly to inoculate survivors against the threat of infection and disease.

With no electricity, Longo cooked what food he could obtain on a barbeque grill and used a little Sterno stove to make coffee. The city water supply was functional within a couple of days, thanks to the use of generators, but residents had to boil water for drinking. A number of good-flowing artesian wells in the immediate vicinity provided another water source. Longo remembered working alongside four local millionaires, unloading beans and other canned goods that had been trucked into the area: "Everybody had their shirts off and dirty—we hadn't bathed in days . . . and just really shoulder to shoulder. If we figured what those men were worth on an hourly basis, it would have been a lot cheaper to send that truck back. But there was no pay and certainly no request for anything—just the opportunity to help people . . . The spirit of the community was unreal—very high . . . We were all kind of reduced to an equal denominator. Folks that sometimes wouldn't talk to other folks became very friendly. It was very good, very nice."

In Pass Christian, Piet and Valena Stegenga mourned the loss of three family members and thanked God their own lives had been saved. Their home and possessions were gone. The post office, a nearby bank, and Ringer's Grocery were gone. They would move in with one of Valena's sisters until they could put their lives back together. Nevertheless, it never dawned on the couple that they would not rebound from the disaster. Said Piet, "I knew in my heart . . . that I'd have more than I ever had in my life . . . I knew in my heart and soul that I was going to bounce back . . . I knew that, I knew that."

Battered Ben Duckworth, stripped of all clothing except a small spandex bathing suit, was in shock. There was a huge gash in one of his thighs, but somehow it had been cauterized by the wind and salt water, possibly saving him from bleeding to death. An old friend, Buddy Jones, spotted Duckworth among the survivors. He quickly commandeered a Navy truck and took him to an emergency facility at the Seabee base in Gulfport, where

Duckworth was treated for his injuries and fell into a deep sleep. Meanwhile, Ben's parents in Jackson, Hubert and Josephine Duckworth, were worried sick. Certain that his son must have died in the wreckage of the Richelieu, Hubert hastily drove to the Coast and began combing through the piles of debris for Ben's body. But as he searched, he encountered Ben's friend and fellow Richelieu survivor, Mike Gannon. "Why, Ben Duckworth isn't dead. I've just seen him and he's all right," said Gannon, much to the relief of Hubert Duckworth.

It would be eight days after the storm before Fritz Gerlach's body would be found perched in the top of a tree near the Richelieu with a mattress on top of him. Mary Ann was too beat up and traumatized to attend his funeral. After spending several weeks in a hospital recovering from her injuries, she would move to Houston, Texas, and then Rockford, Illinois, before settling back on the Mississippi Gulf Coast to begin selling real estate. She said, "Possessions are not worth that much. If I hadn't tried to stay in there and save what I had—my minks and diamonds—my husband would probably be alive." Her life from that point, however, would take a bizarre series of twists.

The afternoon of the storm, Marie Peralta had fled her Pass Christian home with the couple's tenth-grade son and eighth-grade daughter, and they stayed until about 6 o'clock at the home of Gerald's parents about a half block from the beach. Then, they moved over to the home of Gerald's brother on Hiern Avenue. They were accompanied by Marie's mother and stepfather. When the storm surge topped the seawall and washed down Hiern Avenue, a neighbor's house was swept away. The soaked residents of the house, however, were pulled out with ropes and rescued. An oak tree fell onto the home of Gerald's brother, and water blew through the roof and flooded the porch. The house was heavily damaged but was left standing, and everyone inside survived.

The home of Marie's in-laws, however, imploded from the storm's terrific pressure and was washed away. Marie recalled, "It was just like you cleaned off the lot to build a house . . . and the next morning, I walked down by myself to look at his mother's house, and my first impression when I walked out the door was it looked like a town that had been bombed." The house belonging to Marie and Gerald also was gutted, and was left full of mud and debris, but it remained intact. As Marie put it: "After the water leaves, you've got black mud about four to five inches high—stinking black mud that you've got to get out of your house. We had no water, so Jerry ran a hose from the bayou and pumped bayou water into the house." Going without water and other basics in the aftermath of the storm was very depressing to Marie Peralta, but she and her husband were able to bathe in the artesian well at nearby Henderson Point, and she vowed, "I'll never be dirty again." She also observed, "Whether you were rich or poor, you were all in the same boat and we had all been hit hard . . . When people talk to you, they'll say, 'Oh, that happened before Camille' . . . Everything is either before or after Camille."

The U.S. Army's 101st Airborne Division moved into the disaster area, set up mass kitchens and began providing area storm refugees with three square meals a day. The Salvation Army also circulated through the area with food wagons, and the American Red Cross arrived with clothing, blankets, mattresses, and beds. The Mississippi National Guard set up food lines, and clergy and church congregations up and down the Coast did their best to help survivors while nursing their own wounds. Assistance also poured in from cities and counties in neighboring states, including a timely dispatch of aid from Louisiana's Jefferson Parish. The U.S. Army Corps of Engineers and Navy Seabees conducted massive cleanup efforts. There were scattered reports of price-gouging and profiteering in the wake of the storm, but most Gulf Coast residents pitched in and helped one another. Everywhere, American flags popped up in an impromptu show of unity.

In Waveland, Johnny Longo personally suffered "in excess of $50,000" in losses from the hurricane, but could collect only a few hundred dollars from insurance companies, which paid off on damage caused by wind, but not by water. Gulf Coast residents who had flood insurance were few and far between. In nearby Bay St. Louis, Henry Maggio moved into a three-bedroom trailer provided by the government and eventually recouped about 80 percent of his losses.

In Ocean Springs, John Switzer received a $40,000 settlement on his $42,000 loss. Most banks, including Switzer's employer, shut down in the storm's immediate aftermath but were operating again within about a week. Some banks, however, were not as fortunate. At a Pass Christian branch of the Hancock Bank, "the vault was the only thing left standing." Switzer said the Red Cross helped keep the economy afloat by buying disaster relief supplies from local merchants, injecting badly needed dollars into circulation. Everything the Switzer family had possessed, however, except their cars and the clothes on their backs, was gone. Switzer gutted and rewired his house, and pulled out all of the flooring and carpet that was rotten and ruined. "We got the smell out because there wasn't anything left for it to stay in," he said. He obtained an SBA loan at 3 percent, but it would take until 1972 to sell his rebuilt home and it would be 1973 before the Switzers moved into a new home, which they constructed on higher ground.

Robert Taylor spent the night of the 18th with his parents at the Biloxi Holiday Inn, which Taylor's father managed. Then, with some help, he moved back into what was left of his home: "Somewhere, someone gave me some mosquito netting and I found a kerosene lantern, which I filled with lighter fluid, and I was given a small propane stove. I cleared out one room in one area where I had a roof on and I put up my mosquito netting. I found a mattress that wasn't too wet, put it on the floor and lived there until about September 10 or so when young Mitchell Sloan and I found an apartment. By then, I had raked together most of the things that I could find and had the house boarded up. Young Mitch and I lived together until I got my house rebuilt in March and moved back in."

Taylor suffered $80,000 in personal losses and "settled for around $8,000." All that was left of *Morgan 34* was a photo of the racing sloop, which Taylor displayed on a wall of his home years later. He rebuilt and bought new furniture with the aid of an SBA loan, but said his financial investments "all turned to mud." Most of the people who took the brunt of Camille's fury, he noted, lived on the south side of the railroad tracks, which run parallel to U.S. Highway 90 at distances ranging from a quarter to a half mile inland. He said many survivors resented other Gulf Coast residents who had left "on vacation" as the storm approached. Among those who stayed, however, many who still had food in their freezers—but no electricity in the hurricane's aftermath—shared it with others to keep it from spoiling. Taylor said some of the "high-ground people," those who lived north of the railroad tracks, even staged a few "parties" after the storm for the benefit of those survivors left without resources of their own. Most people in his neighborhood moved back in and started rebuilding and those who didn't were considered quitters. "Of course, we're talking about where I live—the long-term Gulfportian and Biloxian had always faced these matters before, in a more limited manner . . . You couldn't get them out with a crowbar," he said. The

Gulf Publishing Company handed out American flags free of charge and Taylor remembered seeing them flying everywhere: "And wherever you saw a flag flying, you knew [they were convinced], 'By God, I had it and I'm staying!' And I was real proud of those people . . . There was a tremendous amount of sympathy for your fellow man . . . The self-discipline of the people was amazing."

Newspaper and television reporters pounced on the Mississippi Gulf Coast in Camille's aftermath like a hungry dog on a bone, seeking out human-interest stories while totaling the material losses in their coverage. Scantily clad Gerald Peralta, still brandishing a revolver on his hip, was persuaded by an NBC-TV news team to stand on the remaining slab of the Richelieu apartments as he was being interviewed on camera. Later, Channel 2 out of Baton Rouge also took him back to the Richelieu for another on-camera interview. The reporter asked him to reenact his movements there the day of the storm as he had tried to persuade the apartment building's residents to leave, and Peralta cooperated: "So I walked up them back steps, and then there was this walkway going out to the swimming pool. Well, that's where I stood, right there on that red tile . . . I looked out there . . . I could see the building, I could see the rails around the building . . . I could see a kid sitting on that blue rug in one of them living rooms. And I don't know what happened to me, but my eyes started watering up—and that man ran over there with a camera and he said, 'That's the best picture I've seen.' But when I walked out there . . . It started coming back to me . . . I've laid awake many a night thinking about it."

As Mississippi governor John Bell Williams toured the devastated Coast, he lingered in what was left of downtown Pass Christian to inspect the damage. Peralta thought he recognized the familiar face and missing arm, and approached Williams. "I had seen pictures of him . . . The governor was leaning up against the police station and I walked up to him and said, 'Governor, how would you like to buy a summer home real cheap?' And he looked at me and the expression—I guess it just hit, you know—and he laughed . . . Like I say, you've got to have a little humor because if you don't, you would go crazy."

His own house wrecked, the police chief initially obtained a 14-foot trailer from his sister for temporary use as the Peralta homestead. He ate most of his meals at nearby Pass Christian High School as he went about his town duties. Subsequently, he secured a 60-foot trailer from HUD for use until he could rebuild his house and move back in the following December. The family used candles until electricity was restored, and hauled water and ice from town to their trailer home for a good month after the storm. Marie remembered: "We got so tired of looking at Vienna sausage and canned Spam . . . that it took many a year before I bought them again . . . You were depressed and there was so much to do . . . You had no clothes to wear . . . And you just didn't know which way to turn at first."

Gerald was confident he and Marie and the kids could rebuild and start over, but he was saddened by the elderly and infirm who had lost everything. He observed, "I would say more people died after Camille because of broken hearts and worries than was actually killed in Camille . . . I mean, you take somebody in their 60s or 70s—and to wipe them out completely so they don't have nothing—that's heartbreaking." Nevertheless, he estimated that 90 percent of the populace rebuilt, and most of them at the same spot. He recalled, "The way that the people more or less stuck together, it was amazing . . . I would say that within two days after the hurricane, you couldn't ride along the beach that you didn't see an American flag flying." And everywhere, there was the obnoxious whine of chain saws. He added, "If you ever want to find out who has been in Camille . . . buy you a chain saw and start it up and watch the expression on their face . . . That's one noise that people will never forget." Johnny Longo agreed. "If you listen to a chain saw long enough, it can get really irritating . . . But I don't guess you can really realize how long we had to listen to chain saws unless you could see the amount of debris that was piled up."

Alma Anderson and her family moved into a vacant apartment immediately after the storm, living in the darkness for a while with no electricity and no television. She walked into the apartment on August 27 and there was a birthday cake with a candle in the middle of it. Everyone inside "started singing 'Happy Birthday'!" As Biloxi began to get back on its feet under the leadership of Mayor Danny Guice, the Andersons sold their property, bought a duplex on Hopkins Boulevard, converted it into a residence, and moved into the structure in 1970. They used an SBA loan to reopen Alma's beauty shop at its previous location in the Trade Winds Hotel. People wondered how Alma, who had a lifelong fear of water, had managed to survive and take everything in stride. Describing Camille as her one and only "baptizing," she attributed her survival and attitude to her faith in God, putting it this way: "I haven't shed a tear about one worldly thing I lost. I told one lady in the shop, 'Look, I had furs, I had diamonds. I had closets full of clothes . . . But when it comes to your life, those things don't mean one thing . . .' And it taught me one thing in life: I don't turn my back on the Lord and what I believe in—and when the chips are down, there's only one person you look to . . . I re-dedicated my life then that if I lived, I was going to do good . . . Well, in fact, I put worldly things behind me and I feel like God was really good to us . . . If you turn your back on God to get everything you can get, it doesn't mean a damn thing." Alma—a onetime queen of the Les Femmes, Les Danseurs Carnival Association— died on September 16, 1998, at the age of 77, and was buried in the Biloxi City Cemetery. Survivors included her husband, Glennan.

Their home and possessions gone, the Stegengas moved in with one of Valena's sisters for a few weeks in the immediate aftermath of Camille. Eventually, the local school system purchased the lot on which their home had stood. Piet took the $3,500 he received for the lot and a

$10,000 SBA loan and used the money to build another home at 823 East Second Street in Pass Christian. They could never replace their lost family members, however, and Valena had nightmares for years afterwards, recalling, "I'd go to bed at night and I'd get to thinking of that water and of that night, and I couldn't sleep."

Edith de Vries never considered abandoning her home and moving away from the Mississippi Coast. She used a walker and then a walking cane to get around, and visited her husband every day in the nursing home until he died about a year after the hurricane. Once she recuperated from her injuries, she resumed an active schedule, and was an avid golfer and gardener a decade later. She remained optimistic, saying, "I'm very happy. I have no complaints, I don't have any resentments, I get along with everybody. My life is just really very lovely. It's all extra. From now on, it's extra."

Lois Toomer battled colon cancer and several other illnesses in the years that followed Camille, as she and her husband rebuilt their home and their lives. Her sister died of heart failure in 1973 and Lois was in an automobile wreck that same year, crushing the right side of her body. She was temporarily forced to wear a colostomy bag following the accident, then underwent a double mastectomy for breast cancer in 1979. Yet, her faith never wavered, and she recounted, "I was lonesome because my sister was dead and I wanted to do for somebody. Life is not worth living if you can't share your life with somebody else . . . Love is the greatest gift you can give away to anyone and I share my love. God has shared it with me."

Robert Taylor underwent surgery in 1970 on the torn cartilage in his right knee, which had been aggravated by his ordeal in Camille. In 1971, he remarried, to a divorced schoolteacher named Marsha who had been a friend of his first wife, and they settled into a house that they built just two blocks from his original home. Robert even bought a new boat, *The Good News*, but sold it in 1977 when a ruptured disk in his back forced him to stop sailing. He got back on his feet financially, however, and also helped establish a bank that same year. Eventually, he came to look at Camille as sort of a "blessing in disguise," in that it forced him to bounce back from the personal problems that had beset him earlier in 1969. He remembered, "It was probably good for me psychologically. It made me make up my mind whether to get back on track or forget about it."

Henry Maggio, who eventually went back to school and became a psychiatrist, noted that the number of divorces in the area where he practiced "probably quadrupled" in the immediate aftermath of Camille, and that suicides and alcoholism increased as a result of depression linked to "storm-related psychic trauma." In Hancock County, he remembered, "A lady who had a problem with alcoholism came outside of her trailer one morning. I can only imagine what was going through her mind, sitting around in all of the destruction, and she shot herself in the head." Maggio avoided the despondency experienced by many survivors by immersing himself in his work and in daily reading and studying of the Bible. He said the scriptures later helped him in his psychiatry practice, explaining, "One of the questions I ask everyone, basically, is what is their relationship with God. I am not interested in their religious denomination. But if I find a depressed person who doesn't have any relationship at all with God, who denies the existence of an Almighty Being, be it whatever we want to call him, I have a sinking feeling that we are not going to get too far . . . There are too many things, such as the storm, that happen in our lives that are greater than we are, that change people's lives . . . That's where God comes into my life and helps me to put things in the proper perspective."

As the Maggio family put their lives back together after the storm, they paused to celebrate his wife's birthday on October 3, 1969, a Saturday. Henry said that it just so happened that there was a "little slab dance that night . . . And that was . . . probably the first time that the socials began to pick up again . . . Of course, the main subject [of conversation] was the storm and what it had done to each of us . . . It's a dividing line in many people's lives."

For the first couple of years after Camille, on the anniversary of the storm, John Switzer and many residents of his Ocean Springs neighborhood dined out—on their driveway, that is. He recalled, "We'd have what we called the 'driveway party' . . . We grabbed a piece of furniture, or a box, or a carton, or something, and sat down on it and opened a can of Vienna sausage and a couple of slices of bread, and a glass of whiskey with some water in it and said, 'Well, I'm glad to be alive.'" He said it cost millions of dollars and took "a year and a half of work by men with barges and tugboats and hydraulic jacks" to get the Biloxi–Ocean Springs bridge into full operation again. After moving back into his rebuilt home, he experienced an eerie uneasiness in the dark of night. He described it this way: "The major psychological thing that got to me—even after we got the house put back together—was going to bed at night, lying down in my bed with the lights off, and the thought would pop into my head unasked: 'Well, John, if water was in this house now like it was in the storm, your head would be three feet under water.' And that hit me every night."

In June 2000, John and his son, John B. Switzer—both of Ocean Springs and the spitting image of each other—won a father-and-son look-alike contest at Biloxi's Edgewater Mall.

The hurricane's grisly death toll in Pass Christian included three women whose bodies were never identified. Dubbed simply Faith, Hope, and Charity, they were buried in gray metal caskets in Gulfport's Evergreen Cemetery. Each year on August 17, Wade Guice and members of his civil defense staff would place flowers on the gravesites and conduct a brief prayer ceremony honoring Camille's victims. Guice continued the practice until his death from cancer in 1996, at which time the Beach Garden Society took over organization of the ceremony. Guice grieved over the hurricane's human toll for the rest of his life, telling an interviewer in 1980, "We lost 132 lives in the storm. I consider each of them a personal failure—and the ghosts of my failures cry out to me every time I drive down the beach, and that's a heavy burden indeed."

Initially, it was generally believed that the interment of Faith, Hope, and Charity marked the final burials of Camille's dead. The last body, however, was yet to be discovered. The crane of a big yellow earth-moving machine plowed into the wreckage of Pass Christian 31 days after the storm, then lurched skyward with a shovel full of muck and rubble. Suddenly, it stopped, and the equipment operator guided his load gently back to the ground, staring blankly at its contents. Protruding from the grisly pile was a human arm. Upon closer inspection, Gerald Peralta, called to the scene, thought he recognized the female victim's dress. Then he was sure. It was the body of Violet McDonald, the 69-year-old mother of a woman Peralta had dated in his younger days. Later, family members positively identified the victim from her rings and other personal belongings.

Peralta worked hand in hand with Pass Christian mayor Joe Wittmann in the aftermath of Camille in an effort to devise a warning system for the city and establish better evacuation routes out of the area. He served as police chief until December of 1974 and subsequently ran unsuccessfully for mayor, losing by three votes. He left politics after that and died in 1982, a little more than three years after his Camille interview and less than a month before his 52nd birthday.

Paul Williams died of cancer on October 11, 1998, at the age of 79. Throughout the remainder of his life after Camille, he grieved over the loss of his wife, 11 of 14 children, and one grandchild in the storm, once telling an interviewer, "I look at their pictures and just wish they were here with me . . . Oh Lordy mercy, nobody knows. Nobody knows how I miss them. This is a painful thing, what I lost. It is real painful and I just have to go around and hold tight and do the best I can. But God knows I miss them so much. I wish they were here."

Members of the Williams family who were killed included his wife, Myrtle M. Williams, 48; children, Floyd, 2, Eddie, 3, Esther, 6, Charles, 7, Clara, 9, Jeremiah, 10, Anna, 11, Sylvester, 15, Deborah, age unknown, Otis, age unknown, 22-year-old married daughter Myrtle Mae Burton; and grandchild Bridget Burton, 5. Another grandchild, William Burton, age unknown, was never accounted for; no records, including obituary or death certificate, could be located for him.

Mary Ann Gerlach, who claimed to be the great-granddaughter of the Confederate general Braxton Bragg, was 31 years of age when she survived Camille. In December of 1992, at age 55, she was released on parole from the Central Mississippi Correctional Facility near Pearl after serving more than 10 years in prison for the January 7, 1981, slaying of her eleventh husband. The victim was Lawrence A. Kietzer, 36, an offshore oil worker whom Gerlach had divorced seven weeks before she shot him five times with a .357-caliber Magnum pistol at the couple's Gulfport home. Gerlach admitted killing Kietzer but blamed the shooting on physical pain and emotional trauma stemming from her experience in Camille. Her marriage to Kietzer, however, did not mark Gerlach's final trip to the altar. She married at least two other men, including her thirteenth husband, James Troy, who also was an inmate at the Rankin County correctional facility where Gerlach was incarcerated. In a series of posthurricane interviews, Gerlach sharply contradicted the testimony of other Richelieu survivors and almost single-handedly perpetuated the myth that a hurricane party was planned or was taking place there the night Camille struck. Ben Duckworth, Rick Keller, and other residents of the apartment complex have vehemently refuted Gerlach's story over the years. In an interview conducted in August of 1979, while she was still married to Kietzer, Mary Ann said, "I don't know what God keeps saving me for, but it seems like he has some purpose."

In August of 2000, Duckworth, then a successful 55-year-old Jackson businessman, returned to his native Gulf Coast to view the Biloxi site of a planned memorial to Camille victims. He also visited the site of the Richelieu, where he found a large Winn-Dixie supermarket doing business. Also gone was the giant oak tree to which Duckworth had clung so tenaciously during his fight for survival.

On August 17, 2001, a crowd gathered on the grounds of the Episcopal Church of the Redeemer in Biloxi to witness the unveiling of a black, polished granite monument etched with the names of Camille's 131 dead and 41 missing. The original church sanctuary was destroyed in the hurricane, but the tall brick bell tower and a flagpole bent during the hurricane remained at the site. Although several Gulf Coast cities have memorials marking the storm, the Hurricane Camille Memorial Wall, which cost $140,000, is the only one honoring victims in all three coastal counties.

Janice Stegenga of Long Beach, daughter-in-law of Piet and Valena Stegenga, lingered following the ceremony and studied the work of Elizabeth Veglia, a mosaic that depicts the eye of Camille. Then, counting each name in the memorial wall behind it, she said, "You see all these names and you realize they are people. We lived in Pass Christian and we lost my husband's grandparents and aunt. The emotion is still there after 32 years." Valena Cuevas Stegenga died in Long Beach on December 4, 2001. She was preceded in death by her husband, Piet.

THE NEXT
CÁMILLE

"It wasn't raining when Noah built the ark," said Wade Guice, "but you've got to get prepared!"

Many residents of the Mississippi Gulf Coast would have welcomed an ark that night of the monster called Camille. Although the Mississippi Coast had been the repeated target of hurricanes over the previous century—with storms reaching landfall within 100 miles of Biloxi at a frequency rate of once every 10 to 15 years—efforts to mitigate against such disasters had been inconsistent and unproductive. Evacuation routes had been poorly planned, with many extending over narrow roads and low-lying bridges that became inundated by storms. Only 50 percent of Harrison County inhabitants evacuated ahead of Camille, leaving more than 50,000 residents of the Coast's most populous county to ride out the hurricane in homes, apartments, nursing homes, emergency shelters, and other vulnerable structures. Neither Harrison County nor one of its cities, Pass Christian, had adopted construction standards prior to Camille.

Growth along the Coast had been uncontrolled and disorganized for 100 years, with few planning and zoning regulations in place. Despite enactment of the National Flood Insurance Program in 1968, implementation of its provisions moved at a snail's pace, and no Mississippi communities were participating in the program in 1969. As Godschalk, Beatley, and Brower noted in their book *Catastrophic Coastal Storms,* "The lack of stronger construction standards required under the program had major impact on the ability of the Harrison County communities to withstand the hurricane." There were no elevation requirements in place for buildings subject to wave action and many were not built to resist hurricane-force winds. Even a house designed by a local architect to be "hurricane proof" was destroyed by Camille, killing the owner and several of his friends who had gathered there to ride out the storm. Their bodies were found many days later. Only a stairway of the house was left standing.

As Camille extended her fingers of destruction three to four blocks inland for the entire length of the Mississippi Coast, homes, apartments, motels, churches, restaurants, schools, and other buildings were swept off their foundations and deposited in piles of debris along with fallen trees, smashed automobiles, remnants of piers, and grounded boats. Some types of buildings withstood the force of wind and water better than others, depending on materials and design. Numerous masonry-block structures did not hold up well and collapsed, as did most piers and boat docks along the Coast. A lot of concrete and steel structures also were demolished. Many wooden structures, however, less rigid and constructed in earlier times with a closer eye to the structural integrity of materials, survived the storm.

Aerial films of the Mississippi coastline taken in the immediate aftermath of Camille survived three decades of neglect before they were discovered by Daniel Lee, owner of Geo Tek Management Services. Originally ordered by NASA and stored away, the films were enhanced by computer techology and are now on display as part of a Camille exhibit at Biloxi's Maritime and Seafood Industry Museum, where Julia Guice, who retired from civil defense work in 1982, now works part-time as a volunteer historic preservationist. The films reveal that "[i]n some places, the debris line—created when trees, piers, houses and businesses become jumbled-up toothpicks—is obvious. In others, the tidal surge is three to five miles inland, much farther than memories recall."

Some modifications to building standards in the region had been made following a couple of earlier severe hurricanes, Audrey in 1957 and Betsy in 1965. One of those modifications, the "open beaches decision," maintained a seawall and artificial sand beach for public use south of Highway 90. Also, after Betsy, Biloxi, Gulfport, and Long Beach adopted the Southern Standard Building

Code. Federal Housing Authority standards were cited as criteria for mortgages, and architects generally used an informal standard of 10 feet above the mean sea level as the elevation guide for new construction. In "Twenty Years After Hurricane Camille: Lessons Learned, Lessons Lost," Pielke, Jr., Simonpietri, and Oxelson noted, "Despite these measures, a uniform building code with hurricane-related stipulations had not been adopted by the coastal counties. Had a code been implemented in the years before Hurricane Camille, the damages would have been less."

Although much of the Gulf beachfront was zoned to remain an open beach for public use after Camille, the property subsequently was manipulated to provide space for marinas, amusement parks, zoos, circuses, carnivals, sports venues, and other uses. A 13.2-foot base elevation was implemented for new construction, and J. E. Maher, director of the Mississippi Emergency Management Agency, warned that construction in low-lying areas and on beaches represented an invitation to property loss. The base elevation at which a new structure would qualify for flood insurance was increased to 21 feet, pushing some structures farther from the water while requiring that others be placed on stilts. "The result is that a hurricane's storm surge . . . floods fewer buildings," Jackson *Clarion-Ledger* reporter James Ricketts wrote in a 1989 article headlined "Hurricane Camille: 20 Years Later." The federal Coastal Zone Management Act of 1972 generated an effort by most coastal states to "manage their shorelines and conserve a vital national resource." Also since that year, Biloxi, Gulfport, Long Beach, Pass Christian, and Harrison County have adopted floodplain ordinances in line with the minimum elevation provisions of the National Flood Insurance Program.

The backbone of Mississippi's shoreline management program, the Wetlands Protection Law of 1973, and enabling legislation of the Mississippi Marine Resources Council, undergird the Mississippi Coastal Program. Charged with enforcement of the program is the state Bureau of Marine Resources, a division of the Department of Wildlife Conservation. Program goals include providing for "reasonable industrial expansion in the coastal area" while conserving "the resources of the coastal area for this and succeeding generations."

The population of Harrison County in 1970, just after Camille, was recorded at 135,000. Biloxi and Gulfport counted about 50,000 residents each, while there were 6,000 in Long Beach and another 3,000 in Pass Christian. The county's tax base was devastated by the storm, and municipal revenues lagged behind operating expenses by some $3.7 million in the two years afterwards.

Within days of the storm, Governor John Bell Williams issued an executive order establishing the Governor's Emergency Council, a blue-ribbon panel intended to oversee cleanup, reconstruction, and redevelopment operations, implement long-range regional planning, and coordinate federal disaster assistance. Said Wade Guice, "The famous one-stop center that you hear so much about was created in Camille . . . It just sort of happened that the agencies got together and said, look, let's all have one representative at one location in each city because people have no automobiles. They don't even have shoes."

The GEC immediately imposed a moratorium on new coastal construction, presented a revised building code, organized a nonprofit coastal building inspection agency, and brought in a consultant to analyze economic development needs. Local government officials, however, resented the council's bureaucratic procedures as an attempt by outsiders to interfere with their own rebuilding efforts and, "[b]y 1971, inspections were being done by the county and the municipalities, a situation that has resulted in problems of code violations . . ." Confusion in the storm's immediate aftermath resulted in unregulated repairs and rebuilding, and the building permit requirement was waived throughout Harrison County. The council's moratorium on new construction was not uniformly enforced and then was lifted before the revised building code proposal could be adopted in final form.

The GEC also solicited a comprehensive study from a Massachusetts company on long-range development in Hancock, Harrison, and Jackson counties. The 324-page study that was delivered to the council examined the history of the Mississippi Coast and suggested solutions for just about every problem the area faced, but little was done to act on proposals contained in the document. According to Ned Boudreaux, manager of transportation planning for the Gulf Regional Planning Commission, "Instead, everyone just took his own piece of property and rebuilt as it was. Local governments were too busy patching streets and repairing sewer systems damaged by the storm to bother coordinating a large-scale development. And residents eager to rebuild their homes and businesses didn't consider their options. Instead of going to new land uses, we just came back and built it stronger."

Opportunities for hazard mitigation were largely ignored in the Gulf Coast's massive rebuilding effort, except for some building code restrictions and elevation requirements mandated by the National Flood Insurance Program. Many areas were rezoned for commercial use, leading to the construction of larger and stronger hotels and restaurants. Gulfport revenues from building permit fees rose by 34 percent in 1969–70, but codes were not enforced in many locations where earlier poor construction of buildings had resulted in their complete destruction. The Camille Project Report, according to Pielke, Jr., Simonpietri, and Oxelson, concluded that Gulf Coast rebuilding efforts could have and should have benefitted from the lessons of Camille:

> The rebuilding of the Mississippi, Louisiana and Alabama Gulf Coasts following Hurricane Camille could have acted as an impetus to develop a coastal community development plan allowing for economic growth and resurgence, guaranteeing preparedness in the event of a repeat storm of equal magnitude. Rather than supporting unchecked

growth with no regard to future hazard mitigation, development could have been steered in a direction that was conscious of the vulnerability of local residents and communities. Hazard mitigation policies might have been adopted at the county or state level, thereby eliminating the discrepancy in level of preparedness between coastal communities.

Nevertheless, President Richard Nixon's prediction that the Gulf Coast would rebuild better than ever was fundamentally fulfilled. Local governments adopted and began to enforce stricter building codes. And, along with the area's rebirth, came news in 1973 that the Coast would get its own early-warning system to help guard against Camilles of the future. Aircraft of the Air Force's 53rd Weather Reconnaissance Squadron, the famous "hurricane hunters," were reassigned from the closed U.S. base at Ramey, Puerto Rico, to Biloxi's Keesler Air Force Base. The 815th Tactical Airlift Squadron also moved to Keesler that same year and, three years later, the unit's mission was changed to weather reconnaissance. The 815th's "storm trackers," manned by reservists of the 403rd Rescue and Weather Reconnaissance Wing, began flying directly into the eyes of developing hurricanes to gather information for use by the National Hurricane Center to forecast the paths and intensity of developing storms. The Federal Emergency Management Agency was authorized by the Disaster Relief Act of 1974 to work with local communities and states to establish disaster preparedness plans or augment those already in place. Yet, hurricane evacuation remained a critical problem on barrier islands and coastal floodplains. In *Living with the Alabama-Mississippi Shore*, Canis, Neal, Pilkey, Jr., and Pilkey, Sr., note that "Due to heavy concentrations of population in areas of low elevation, narrow roads and vulnerable bridges and causeways, plus limited hurricane warning capability (possibly 12 hours or less), it may be difficult to evacuate all people prior to a hurricane."

By 1979, the Mississippi Coast had been resurrected. To be sure, stairs to nowhere and slabs where buildings had once stood were clearly visible to motorists traveling along Highway 90. The seawall, sand beach, and scenic drive down the busy thoroughfare, however, had been rebuilt and landscaped. Tourism flourished more than ever amid the glitter and twinkle of busy motels, restaurants, and souvenir shops. The familiar Baricev's Restaurant was back in operation on Biloxi's beachfront, and a brand-new Coast Coliseum added an imposing presence to the landscape between Biloxi and Gulfport. The people of the Coast had pulled together in the aftermath of Camille, and with the reconstruction had come new opportunities for businesses to move, repair, modernize, or, in some cases, gracefully close their doors for good. The Camille relief effort had pumped new dollars into the local economy, new railroad bridges spanned the bays of Biloxi and Bay St. Louis, and, according to Biloxi oil man Tommy Munro, "new industry sprang from the chaos and confusion of the storm's aftermath." Hancock Bank officials figured that more than $488 million fueled the Coast economy after Camille—exclusive of the untold contributions of food, supplies, and other help from the Salvation Army and other relief agencies. Chevis Swetman, president of The People's Bank of Biloxi, maintained that the hurricane recovery effort kept the Coast out of a nationwide recession, as "building-related businesses and banks grew."

While thousands of Harrison County residents had declined to evacuate in advance of Camille, the county's coastal area was "one-hundred percent evacuated during Hurricane Frederic in 1979." Only a decade removed from Camille, Gulf Coast residents were keenly aware of what a hurricane could do and respected that terrible power. A countering impact on the human psyche, however, according to Godschalk and others, was that Camille was perceived by many "as a once-in-a-lifetime event which cannot be planned for or mitigated. Residents believe that nothing can survive another storm of this same force, leading them toward an anti-hazard mitigation attitude." Although critical to storm mitigation efforts, attempts by regional, state, and federal authorities to impose land-use regulations, which might have improved planning by the coastal counties, proved politically unpopular. In 1984, a 69-unit condominium was constructed at Henderson Point—on land that had been leveled by Camille.

After Camille, it would be 20 years before another storm of Category 4 strength would hit the U.S. mainland—Hurricane Hugo in 1989. The nation's third and most recent Category 5 storm, Hurricane Andrew, followed in 1992. During the closing decades of the twentieth century, however, tremendous growth took place along U.S. coastlines as millions of Americans went in hot pursuit of sun, sand, and surf. Increasingly, land developers and homeowners built or rebuilt in areas critically vulnerable to Mother Nature's inevitable wrath from the sea. As hurricane forecasts became more accurate, the actual length of the U.S. coastline "increased from less than 300 nautical miles in the late 1960s to about 400 nautical miles" from 1989 to 1999.

Consider that only 150,000 people were ordered to evacuate during the approach of Camille and compare that with the 750,000 ordered to evacuate as Andrew approached the more populous area in south Florida. Population density complicates evacuation plans, necessitating longer lead time from warning to storm and ensuring traffic jams of unprecedented proportions as those caught in the path of the storm seek refuge. More development also means more property is at greater risk, leading Pielke and Pielke to conclude: "A direct hit of a storm like Camille on Miami or New Orleans [today] could exceed $80 billion." New Orleans, of course—located below sea level and practically surrounded by water—is particularly vulnerable.

Notwithstanding the Mississippi Gulf Coast's amazing resurgence during the two decades after Camille, hardly anyone could have predicted the area's total transformation that would take place in the 1990s with the advent of legalized gambling. The state legislature's enactment of a riverboat gambling act in 1990 set the stage for the eruption of a multimillion-dollar beachfront and bayside casino industry in Harrison and Hancock counties. Only Jackson County excluded itself from gaming profits, as casinos and their adjacent high-rise hotels took over the sites of local restaurants such as Baricev's and the Sea 'n Sirloin and other business establishments that had been familiar landmarks for many years along the south side of Highway 90. Bernard Goldstein moved his casino business interests from Iowa to Mississippi, and his Casino America, Inc., became "the first publicly traded riverboat casino operator in the country." Determined to find a symbolic link to local history for his new casino, Goldstein was reminded of the Isle of Caprice, an old Prohibition-era gambling hall that had flourished for a time on Dog Island south of Biloxi. He shortened Caprice to Capri and soon became board chairman and CEO of Isle of Capri Casinos, Inc. The Isle of Capri Casino Resort became the Gulf Coast's first casino, setting up operations in Biloxi in 1992. Since state law required casinos to be located on water and since the Mississippi Gulf Coast already was a popular waterfront tourist attraction, the area soon became home to at least a dozen casinos, including nine in Biloxi, two in Gulfport, and one on the back bay of St. Louis. Said Larry Gregory, director of the Mississippi Gaming Commission, in a 2002 *Mississippi Business Journal* article by Becky Gillette: "Literally, the Gulf Coast took a gamble and voted to legalize gaming in

Harrison and Hancock counties. Ten years later, we can proudly say that gamble paid off."

The gaming success some dubbed the "Mississippi Miracle" produced an offshoot of first-class hotels, restaurants, and entertainment venues to complement tourist interests centering around crap tables, slot machines, and roulette wheels. Cars and recreational vehicles bearing license tags from all across the country began showing up in large numbers as the Gulf Coast—with its deep-sea fishing charters, rich history, and New Orleans–style cuisine—matured at last into a resort destination, rather than a destination of last resort. Large successful companies such as Grand Casino and Casino Magic took their place alongside other casinos such as New Palace, Boomtown, Imperial Palace, Treasure Bay, and President. Then, in March of 1999, came the Beau Rivage with its $700 million, 1,780-room casino and hotel investment. Casinos fueled Harrison County's population growth from about 165,000 in 1990 to a conservative estimate of nearly 200,000 by 2000. Hotel rooms and single-family housing starts "roughly tripled to about 17,000 and 2,610, respectively, from the early 1990s to 1999." The expansion today continues full throttle. In 2003, the Isle of Capri announced plans for an $80 million construction project that was to include a 400-room hotel tower and a 1,116-car parking garage. According to Gillette, Biloxi mayor A. J. Holloway began referring to the Coast's dramatic transformation as "the nation's Cinderella story," adding, "We have gone from about . . . eleven million dollars [in tourist business before casinos] to twenty-five million dollars a year [after casinos] . . . We have gone from 4,000 hotel rooms to 17,000 today in Biloxi. We have added daily jet service and have seen the airport go from 185,000 passengers a year before casinos to almost a million passengers in recent years. And we have seen the coliseum and convention center double the size of its meeting space."

In just a handful of years, Mississippi, with its Gulf Coast casinos and a string of additional gambling establishments stretching along the Mississippi River from Natchez to Memphis, became the nation's third-leading gaming destination, trailing only Las Vegas and Atlantic City. With gaming tax revenues reaching $320 million a year, plus another $40 million in corollary tax revenues, the casino industry contributed between 7 and 10 percent of the state's annual budget. The new tax dollars had an amazing impact on all elements of the city of Biloxi, providing $80 million for public works improvements and $60 million for upgrading transportation infrastructure, creating jobs, improving recreational and educational facilities, boosting staff and training for police and fire departments, and even supporting historic preservation efforts. Gaming taxes helped build Biloxi's new $32 million high school and pumped another $20 million into other school construction projects. High rollers and low rollers alike, in partnership with state and local governments, generally improved the quality of life for Gulf Coast citizens. "Biloxi is now one of the fastest growing areas in the country and stands poised to become an internationally renowned destination resort," observed Edmond Bodreaux, Jr., in "Mississippi Gulf Coast Native Americans."

The hurricane is a terrible force of nature, unrivaled in ferocity except, perhaps, by earthquakes and rare volcanic eruptions. Here today, gone tomorrow. Despite humanity's terrible experiences throughout the ages, hurricanes continue to test the limits of modern meteorological science. No other natural calamity is so consistently relentless in its assault on the civilized and the uncivilized world. Deriving their power from the solar energy of hot tropical oceans, they are the ultimate storm. Hurricane Georges in 1999 "released enough heat energy in a few short weeks to power the electrical needs of the United States for a decade." Hurricane forecasting, always an inexact science, is complicated by rapid and erratically moving storms, and experts say only marginal improvements in predicting their course and intensity can be expected in the future. While the loss of life associated with hurricanes has declined in recent history, death tolls in the future may rise as people flock to coastal areas in increasing numbers and evacuation problems intensify. Property losses also may skyrocket. "Meanwhile, the anticipated rise in sea level could cause severe increases in coastal erosion over the next 30 to 40 years, leaving much existing development awash," Godschalk, Beatley, and Brower warned.

At every opportunity, hurricane researchers are dropping temperature and weather probes into the storms in an effort to better determine where they will hit and how hard. Scientists from the National Oceanic and Atmospheric Administration, National Aeronautics and Space Administration, the University of Miami, and the U.S. Air Force want to know the speed of their surface winds, where they will make landfall, and how warm-water currents provide the energy that allows the storms to intensify. "For coastal residents and business owners, that means earlier and better targeted evacuations, an increasingly important factor in densely populated coastal communities where 24 hours is no longer enough time to safely evacuate," Associated Press reporter Vickie Chachere wrote in 2001.

The 2002 hurricane season saw a dozen tropical storms (two more than average) and four hurricanes (two fewer than average). Although it was the quietest year since El Niño weather patterns suppressed hurricane activity in 1997, a record eight storms formed during September, and the Mississippi Gulf Coast did not escape damage. Tropical Storm Isidore, September 14–26, battered piers on the beachfront in Harrison County and dumped heavy rains that sparked flooding in Hancock County, causing an estimated $5 million in damage. Hurricane Lili, September 21–October 4, reached Category 4 status as it neared the Louisiana coastline, but the storm's 145-mile-per-hour winds and threatening storm surge subsided dramatically before it made landfall and pushed inland—again affecting the Mississippi Coast in the same areas where Isidore had struck a week earlier.

Some 6,300 storm victims pelted the Federal Emergency Management Agency with damage claims totaling more than $17 million in the aftermath of Isidore and Lili. Mississippi Gulf Coast casinos lost $8 million in anticipated revenue and some of the gaming establishments were banged up by the storms. Isidore caused about $2.5 million in damage to the Grand Casino in Gulfport and the Grand Bear golf course just north of the city. An entrance ramp was torn away at Treasure Bay Casino in Biloxi, leaving a 12-foot gash in the gambling barge.

Civil defense officials in the three coastal counties had been running public service announcements for the two previous years in an effort to make residents aware of the evacuation zones in which they lived. Maps of the zones were available at the courthouses and city halls of each Gulf Coast municipality, and the information also was posted on civil defense Web sites. If Coast residents had been paying attention, many probably would not have been forced out of their homes by Isidore's floodwaters. A frustrated Linda Rouse, Harrison County civil defense director, told Biloxi *Sun Herald* reporter Melissa Scallan in 2002, "I don't know how else to get the word out." Julia Guice maintains that state highway 15 from Biloxi to Laurel should be four-laned to dilute the northward emergency traffic flow that now would be almost totally dependent on U.S. Highway 49. In April 2002, the Mississippi Emergency Management Agency, which has statutory authority to coordinate the development and implementation of the state's emergency management activities, hosted seven public meetings on the Gulf Coast and in the Interstate 59 corridor counties stretching northward from the Louisiana state line. The Mississippi Department of Transportation proposed an I-59 contraflow plan that would create at least three northbound lanes of traffic out of four lanes along the busy highway to speed evacuation of storm-threatened refugees. Mississippi governor Ronnie Musgrove and Louisiana governor Mike Foster also vowed to work together to develop a more comprehensive evacuation plan to help protect the citizens of both states from hurricanes and other natural disasters.

It may seem overly simplistic to propose that the most effective storm mitigation strategy would be to manage the growth and development of coastal areas to keep as many people as possible out of harm's way. Certainly, studies have shown that state governments can "play vital roles in promoting safer patterns of coastal development." A quick reality check, however, confirms that any move toward restricted coastal development would require a major commitment of will, resources, and cooperation at all levels of government—federal, state, and local. Hurricane Camille taught us lessons more than three decades ago, as did Hurricane Andrew just a little over one decade ago. The knowledge and experience gained from hurricane history, however, have not necessarily translated into changes in behavioral patterns or produced practical actions that would keep the disasters of the past from repeating themselves. Indeed, the nation's vulnerability to hurricanes increases in proportion to the increasing development of coastal areas. Short-term societal responses before and after hurricanes should be based upon decisions and policies made over the long term. As the Camille Project Report stated: "Hurricane Camille, like every storm, provides a real-world test of the existing level of preparedness. Without exception, each storm reveals areas where society could have been better prepared or less vulnerable. If we are to identify those actions needed to improve a community's preparation for hurricane impacts, then we must focus attention on ways to ascertain a community's exposure BEFORE a hurricane strikes."

The thirtieth anniversary of Camille in 1999 provided an opportune time to raise the issue of a national hurricane policy and consider policy actions that might better prepare the country for the "inevitable Camilles of the future." A national policy, however, has not emerged. Jay Barnes wrote, "There is little doubt about it—sooner or later, another big hurricane will come. Atmospheric scientists and emergency planners agree that it's just a matter of time . . . The question is: Are we ready for the next great hurricane?" The stakes are certainly much higher now. Where and when will another monster storm strike? No one knows for sure.

It may be worth remembering, however, that Dog Island and the Isle of Caprice have long since vanished beneath the dark and murky waters of the Mississippi Sound, where perhaps only the ghosts of 1930s revelers cavort in the shadowy depths of a gamblers' playground that is no more.

NOTES

"YOU COULD SEE THE BLACK COMING IN"

Chapter one is based largely on interviews with Hurricane Camille survivors conducted a decade or more after the storm by R. Wayne Pyle of the Mississippi Oral History Program at the University of Southern Mississippi. Those interviewed included: Wade Guice, former longtime Harrison County civil defense director; Gerald Peralta, former police chief at Pass Christian; Dr. Henry Maggio, a Bay St. Louis physician; Robert Lawrence Taylor, a Gulfport attorney; Alma Anderson of Biloxi; Lois Toomer of Gulfport; Edith de Vries of Pass Christian; Mary Ann Gerlach, a former resident of the Richelieu Manor apartment complex in Pass Christian; Paul Williams, Sr., former caretaker of the Trinity Episcopal Church in Pass Christian; Piet Stegenga and Valena Stegenga of Pass Christian; and John Longo, Jr., former mayor of Waveland. Additional information was compiled from the recollections of Gregory Durrschmidt, who was an airman stationed at Keesler Air Force Base in Biloxi at the time of Camille, and from an e-mail message to the author from Richelieu survivor Richard C. Keller, whose wife perished in the storm. Other contributions included newspaper reports written by Kat Bergeron, Thomas Bevier, Wyatt Emmerich, John Maines, and Danny McKenzie.

"expected to move": Sullivan 93.
"begin quietly": Bergeron, "Blast from the Past," E2.

"the lowest sea level pressure": "The Story of Hurricane Camille," 2.

"the black-and-yellow signs": Bergeron, "Camille Survivors Want Truth to be Had," A3.

"Never before": Sullivan 96.

"Many not only": Sullivan 97.

"But radio reports": Bevier.

"Luane said": Emmerich A4.

"was nothing but wood": Emmerich A4.

"that probably saved": Bergeron, "Camille Survivors Want Truth to be Had," A3.

THE HISTORY OF THE
MISSISSIPPI GULF COAST

This chapter draws heavily from the work of Val Husley, *Biloxi: 300 Years*; Edmond Boudreaux, Jr., "Mississippi Gulf Coast Native Americans"; Charles Sullivan, *Hurricanes of the Mississippi Gulf Coast*; Dave D. Davis, ed., *Perspectives on Gulf Coast Prehistory*; Mike Hobbs, "Mississippi's Offshore Islands"; Richebourg Gaillard McWilliams, ed., *Iberville's Gulf Journals*; Rebecca Larche Moreton, "The French Language of the Coast"; Richard Glaczier, "The History of Gulf Coast Hurricanes"; Dan Ellis, "Bay St. Louis, Waveland, and Diamondhead," "Hancock County and Unincorporated Communities," "Henderson Point," "The Sullivan-Ryan Fight," and "Cat Island"; Mary Ellen Alexander, "Long Beach, Mississippi"; Steve Dickerson and Jim Miller, "City of Gulfport"; Ray Bellande, "A History of Ocean Springs, Mississippi"; Murella Hebert Powell, "Biloxi, Queen City of the Gulf Coast"; and a University of Southern Mississippi oral history interview with Wade Guice.

"deep water": Hobbs 2:3.

"Three of those": McWilliams 44.

"annexed the region": Husley 27.

"Pirate House": Ellis 1:23.

"Unannexable": Ellis 1:1.

"playground": Ellis 1:67–71.

"dueling oaks": Ellis 1:73.
"Bear Point": Alexander 1:79.
"Little Italy": Alexander 1:93.
"strewn with pine trees": Husley 37.
"no-man's land": Sullivan 28.
"as if ashamed": Sullivan 29.
"Seafood Capital": Sullivan 29.
"was directly connected": Powell 1:144.
"the new deep-water": Powell 1:145.
"caused considerable": Powell 1:145.
"set a new record": Sullivan 44.
"a barometric reading": Sullivan 53.
"off his marble": Sullivan 61.
"For the sixth time": Sullivan 63.
"reportedly the longest": Husley 118.
"the ambiance"; Husley 124.
"By 1930": Sullivan 66.
"was heralded": Husley 129.
"declared Florida": Sullivan 83.
"Longest-man-made beach": Husley 142.

HUNRÁKEN

Chapter three relies heavily on the work of Edward N. Rappaport and Jose Fernandez, "The Deadliest Atlantic Tropical Cyclones, 1492–Present"; Roger A. Pielke, Jr., and Roger A. Pielke, Sr., *Hurricanes: Their Nature and Impacts on Society*, *The Hurricane*, and "What Can We Learn from Andrew?"; Roger A. Pielke, Jr., Chantal Simonpietri, and Jennifer Oxelson, "Twenty Years after Hurricane Camille: Lessons Learned, Lessons Lost"; Jay Barnes, *Florida's Hurricane History* and "Jay Barnes on Hurricanes: The Next Great Storm"; Eric Sloane, *The Book of Storms*; Jeffrey Rosenfeld, *Eye of the Storm: Inside the World's Deadliest Hurricanes, Tornadoes and Blizzards*; Dr. Hal Gerrish, "The Deadliest U.S. Hurricanes of This Century," "Hurricanes: General Background," and "The Most Intense U.S. Hurricanes of This Century";

Ivan Ray Tannehill, *Hurricanes*; and David R. Godschalk, Timothy Beatley, and David J. Brower, *Catastrophic Coastal Storms*.

"forever changed": "The Grand Isle Hurricane (1909)," 1.
"caused Lake Pontchartrain": "The 1915 New Orleans Hurricane," 1.
"There were so many": "Horrific Labor Day Storm of 1935," 1.
"nightmare scenario": "Labor Day Hurricane of 1935," 1.
"costliest hurricane": Pielke and Pielke 2, "What Can We Learn from Andrew?"
"these delicately": Ross 37.
"seasonal cyclones": Barnes 6.
"turn-to-the-right law": Sloane 16.
"If an adequate": Rosenfeld 273.
"a three-fold increase": "Overview of Atlantic Hurricanes," 1.
"set a record": Barnes 28.
"divorce itself": Sloane 13.
"Kyklon": Ross 17.
"Feminists urged": "Overview of Atlantic Hurricanes," 2.
"Names of outstanding": "Hurricanes: General Background," 21.
"values are highly": "Saffir-Simpson Hurricane Scale," 1.
"Terrain lower": "Saffir-Simpson Hurricane Scale," 2.
"all structures": "Saffir-Simpson Hurricane Scale," 2.
"With the exception": "Category 5 Monsters," 3.
"three times": "Category 5 Monsters," 3.
"verify his theory": Barnes 33.
"helped to clarify": Rappaport 2.
"accurate wind records": Barnes 17.
"to have had": Barnes 33.
"received in time": Rappaport 4.
"responsibility to track": Barnes 33–34.
"perishable balloons": "Overview of Atlantic Hurricanes," 1–2.
"Dvorak technique": Gerrish, "Hurricanes: General Background," 4.
"dropwindsones": Gerrish, "Hurricanes: General Background," 4.
"document vertical profiles": Gerrish, "Hurricanes: General Background," 4.
"With the growth": Godschalk , Beatley, and Brower 14.
"magnet for storms": "All About Hurricanes," 1.

KILLER CAMILLE

Chapter four is based almost entirely on interviews conducted by R. Wayne Pyle of the University of Southern Mississippi's Oral History Program a decade or more after Camille with the following survivors: Robert Lawrence Taylor, Dr. Henry Maggio, Alma Anderson, Gerald Peralta, Piet Stegenga and Valena Stegenga, Paul Williams, Sr., Mary Ann Gerlach, Edith de Vries, John Longo, Jr., Wade Guice, Lois Toomer, John A. Switzer of Ocean Springs, Fred DeMetz of Pass Christian, Richard Merritt of Pass Christian, and Charles Webb, former golf pro at the Broadwater Beach Hotel in Biloxi. Other materials were supplied by Charles Sullivan, *Hurricanes of the Mississippi Gulf Coast*; the recollections of Gregory Durrschmidt; and an e-mail message to the author from Richelieu survivor Richard C. Keller.

"amid the sounds": Sullivan 104.
"Will we survive": Bergeron, "Camille Survivors Want Truth to be Had," A3.
"like a zipper": Bergeron, "Camille Survivors," A3.
"slow elevator ride": Emmerich A4.
"She's gone": Bergeron, "Camille Survivors," A3.

TRACKING THE MONSTER

This chapter draws extensively from the work of Charles Sullivan and Roger A. Pielke, Jr., previously cited; Herbert J. Thompson, "The James River Flood of August 1969 in Virginia"; Jerry DeLaughter, "Ten Years After Camille"; and newspaper accounts written by Kat Bergeron, Steve Brunsman, and George Lammons.

"difference between": "USA's Second Straight 20th Century Hurricane," 1.
"Material things": Brunsman B2.
"It looked like": Brunsman B2.
"That's when it hit me": Brunsman B1.
"the wind was blowing": "Lack of Lights an Eerie Feeling," H1.

"eerie feeling": "Lack of Lights an Eerie Feeling," H1.
"a little more than": Pielke, Jr., Simonpietri, and Oxelson, "Twenty
    Years After Hurricane Camille: Lessons Learned, Lessons Lost," 7.
"flourished in the intense": "Hurricane Camille: Aug. 17, 1969," 6.
"The hurricane pulled": DeLaughter 25.

THE SURVIVORS

Chapter six is based upon the recollections of Gregory Durrschmidt;
newspaper reports written by Kat Bergeron and Wyatt Emmerich; and
University of Southern Mississippi oral history interviews by R. Wayne
Pyle with Fred DeMetz, Dorothy Niolet, Richard Merritt, John A.
Switzer, Alma Anderson, Charles Webb, Robert Lawrence Taylor, Lois
Toomer, Edith de Vries, Dr. Henry Maggio, John Longo, Jr., Piet Ste-
genga and Valena Stegenga, Gerald Peralta and Marie Peralta, Paul
Williams, Sr., and Wade Guice.

"Why, Ben Duckworth": Emmerich A4.
"You see all these": Bergeron, "Wall's Roll Honors Victims," A8.

THE NEXT CAMILLE

Chapter seven includes the contributions of David R. Godschalk, Tim-
othy Beatley, and David J. Brower, and Charles Sullivan, Edmond
Boudreaux, Jr., Jeffrey Rosenfeld, Roger A. Pielke, Jr., and Jay Barnes,
all previously cited; Edward N. Akin and Charles C. Bolton, *Mississippi:
An Illustrated History*; Wayne F. Canis, William J. Neal, Orrin H. Pilkey,
Jr., and Orrin H. Pilkey, Sr., *Living with the Alabama-Mississippi Shore*;
and newspaper reports written by James Ricketts, Sharon Stallworth,
George Lammons, Becky Gillette, Vickie Chachere, and Melissa
Scallan.

"It wasn't raining": Ricketts, "If Camille II Hits, Gulf Coast Will Be Bet-
    ter Prepared," 1.

"In some places": "Forgotten Films Unlock Mysteries," A11.

"open beaches decision": Pielke, Jr., Simonpietri, and Oxelson, "Twenty Years after Hurricane Camille: Lessons Learned, Lessons Lost," 10.

"manage their shorelines": Canis et al. 130.

"reasonable industrial": Canis et al. 130.

"By 1971": Godschalk, Beatley, and Brower 58.

"The rebuilding": Pielke, Jr., Simonpietri, and Oxelson, "Twenty Years After Hurricane Camille," 14.

"storm trackers": Sullivan 118.

"new industry": Lammons C3.

"building-related": Lammons C3.

"one-hundred percent": Godschalk, Beatley, and Brower 60.

"increased from less": Pielke, Jr., Simonpietri, and Oxelson, "Twenty Years After Hurricane Camille," 16.

"the first publicly traded": Akin 186.

"Mississippi Miracle": Gillette 34.

"roughly tripled": "With So Much to Lose, Coast Must Not Forget," C8.

"released enough heat": Rosenfeld 225.

"play vital roles": Godschalk, Beatley, and Brower 252.

"inevitable Camilles": Pielke, Jr., Simonpietri, and Oxelson, "Twenty Years After Hurricane Camille," 6.

WORKS CITED

Akin, Edward N., and Charles C. Bolton. *Mississippi: An Illustrated History*. Sun Valley: American Historical Press, 2002.

Alexander, Mary Ellen. "Long Beach, Mississippi." In *Marine Resources and History of the Mississippi Gulf Coast: History, Art, and Culture of the Mississippi Gulf Coast*. 2 vols. Mississippi Department of Marine Resources, 1998.

"All About Hurricanes." Introduction (Novenas). *Virtually New Orleans*, copyright 1995, 1996, Yatcom Communications, Inc., 3 June 2002. http://www.yatcom.com/neworl/weather/hurricane.html.

"Backgrounder: Hurricanes." *Federal Emergency Management Agency Library*, 3 June 2002. http://www.fema.gov/library/hurrica.htm.

Barnes, Jay. *Florida's Hurricane History*. Chapel Hill and London: University of North Carolina Press, 1998.

———. "Jay Barnes on Hurricanes: The Next Great Storm." *North Carolina's Hurricane History*. 3rd ed. Chapel Hill: University of North Carolina Press, 2001. UNC Press Online, 3 June 2002. http://www.ibiblio.orgluncpress/hurricanes/great_storm.html.

"Basics: Origin and Life Cycle." *National Oceanic and Atmospheric Administration*, 26 February 2002. http://hurricanes.noaa.gov/prepare/origin.htm.

Bellande, Ray. "A History of Ocean Springs, Mississippi." In *Marine Resources and History of the Mississippi Gulf Coast: History, Art and Culture of the Mississippi Gulf Coast*. 2 vols. Mississippi Department of Marine Resources, 1998.

Bergeron, Kat. "Blast from the Past: Summer '69. Coast Caught the Wave of '69." Biloxi *Sun Herald*, 16 July 1989, E1+.

———. "Camille Survivors Want Truth to Be Had." Biloxi *Sun Herald*, 17 Aug. 2000, A1+.

———. "Camille Was No Lady. Storm of the Century. Hurricane Camille: 20 Years Later." Biloxi *Sun Herald*, 13 Aug. 1989, E9.

———. "Faith, Hope, Charity Not Forgotten." Biloxi *Sun Herald*, 18 Aug. 2001, A8.

———. "Finally, Camille Dead Can Be Put to Rest." Biloxi *Sun Herald*, 12 Aug. 2001, G1+.

———. "Forgotten Films Unlock Mysteries." Biloxi *Sun Herald*, n.d., A1+.

———. "Friendship Oak Helps Replant Coast Trees. Storm of the Century. Hurricane Camille: 20 Years Later." Biloxi *Sun Herald*, 13 Aug. 1989, E10.

———. "Gone But Not Forgotten. Storm of the Century. Hurricane Camille: 20 Years Later." Biloxi *Sun Herald*, 13 Aug. 1989, F1.

———. "Wall's Roll Honors Victims." Biloxi *Sun Herald*, 18 Aug. 2001, A1+

Bevier, Thomas. "Pass Christian Apartment Dweller Denies Party." Memphis *Commercial Appeal*, 9 Sept. 1969.

Bixel, Patricia Bellis, and Elizabeth Hays Turner. *Galveston and the 1900 Storm: Catastrophe and Catalyst*. Austin: University of Texas Press, 2000.

Boudreaux, Edmond, Jr. "Mississippi Gulf Coast Native Americans." In *Marine Resources and History of the Mississippi Gulf Coast: History, Art, and Culture of the Mississippi Gulf Coast*. 2 vols. Mississippi Department of Marine Resources, 1998.

———. "Biloxi, Pascagoula, Acolapissa, and Capinan Indians." In *Marine Resources and History of the Mississippi Gulf Coast: History, Art, and Culture of the Mississippi Gulf Coast*. 2 vols. Mississippi Department of Marine Resources, 1998.

———. "Biloxi—Past and Present." Biloxi Chamber of Commerce, 7 Jan. 2003. http//:biloxi.org/past.shtml.

Brown, Timothy. "Lili, Isidore Hit Same Areas on Coast." Jackson *Clarion-Ledger*, 18 Oct. 2002.

Brunsman, Steve. "Camille Paid No Respect to Religion. Houses of Worship Disappear." Biloxi *Sun Herald*, 19 Aug. 1989, B1+.

"Camille Remembered with Bent Flag Pole." Biloxi *Sun Herald*, 18 Aug. 2000, A1.

Canis, Wayne F., William J. Neal, Orrin H. Pilkey, Jr., and Orrin H. Pilkey, Sr. *Living with the Alabama-Mississippi Shore.* Durham: Duke University Press, 1985.

"Category 5 Monsters." *National Climatic Data Center.* NCDC: Satellite Events Arts Gallery/Educational Topics, 3 June 2002. http://lwf.ncdc.noaa.gov/oa/satellite/satelliteseye/educational/cat5hur.html.

Chachere, Vickie. "Scientists Seek Better Data on Hurricanes." The Associated Press, Tampa, 16 Aug. 2001.

Davis, Dave D., ed. *Perspectives on Gulf Coast Prehistory.* Gainesville: University Presses of Florida, 1984.

"The Deadliest, Costliest and Most Intense U.S. Hurricanes of this Century." *The National Hurricane Center, National Oceanic and Atmospheric Administration,* NOAA Technical Memorandum NWS TPC-1, Feb. 1997: 3 June 2002. http://www.nhc.noaa.gov/pastdead.html.

DeAngelis, Richard M. "Enter Camille." *Weatherwise,* Oct. 1969: 176, Environmental Data Service, ESSA, Washington, D.C. Infotrieve, Inc., University of Southern Mississippi Cook Library. service@infotrieve.com.

DeLaughter, Jerry. "Ten Years After Camille." *The South Magazine,* July 1979, 25.

Dickerson, Steve, and Jim Miller. "City of Gulfport." In *Marine Resources and History of the Mississippi Gulf Coast: History, Art, and Culture of the Mississippi Gulf Coast.* 2 vols. Mississippi Department of Marine Resources, 1998.

Durrschmidt, Gregory. "Paradise Lost: Hurricane Camille Capped a Turbulent Summer of '69." *Weatherwise* 52 (1999): 32–37.

Ellis, Dan. "Bay St. Louis, Waveland, and Diamondhead." In *Marine Resources and History of the Mississippi Gulf Coast: History, Art, and Culture of the Mississippi Gulf Coast.* 2 vols. Mississippi Department of Marine Resources, 1998

———. "Cat Island." In *Marine Resources and History of the Mississippi Gulf Coast: Mississippi's Coastal Environment.* 2 vols. Mississippi Department of Marine Resources, 1998.

———. "Hancock County and Unincorporated Communities." In *Marine Resources and History of the Mississippi Gulf Coast: History, Art, and Culture of the Mississippi Gulf Coast.* 2 vols. Mississippi Department of Marine Resources, 1998.

———. "Henderson Point." In *Marine Resources and History of the Mississippi Gulf Coast: History, Art, and Culture of the Mississippi Gulf Coast.* 2 vols. Mississippi Department of Marine Resources, 1998.

———. "The Sullivan-Ryan Fight."In *Marine Resources and History of the Mississippi Gulf Coast: History, Art, and Culture of the Mississippi Gulf Coast.* 2 vols. Mississippi Department of Marine Resources, 1998.

Emmerich, Wyatt. "Now Here's a Real Hurricane Story." Jackson *Northside Sun*, 13 Sept. 1992, A4.

"The Florida/Mississippi Hurricane (1947)." *Storm Signals Online*, 25 Feb. 2002. http://www.stormsignals.com/1947.htm.

"Galveston Hurricane, Sept. 8–9, 1900." *Climate-Watch*, National Climatic Data Center, Sept. 2000. National Oceanic and Atmospheric Administration, 3 June 2002. http://lwf.ncdc.noaa.gov/oa/climate/extremes/2000/september/extremes0900.htm.

"Georges Pummels Caribbean, Florida Keys, and the U.S. Gulf Coast." *National Climatic Data Center*, 12 Apr. 1999, 3 June 2002. http://lwf.ncdc.noaa.gov/oa/reports/georges/georges.html.

Gerrish, Dr. Hal. "The Deadliest U.S. Hurricanes of This Century." *Earthlink*, 9 Sept. 1998. http://home.earthlink.net/~hurricanehal/hurricanefacts.html.

———. "Hurricanes: General Background." *Earthlink*, 9 Sept. 1998. http://home.earthlink.net/hurricanehal.hurricanes.htm.

———. "The Most Intense U.S. Hurricanes of This Century." *Earthlink*, 9 Sept. 1998. http://home.earthlink.nete/~hurricanehal/hurricanefacts.html.

Gillette, Becky. "Big Gamble for the Coast Leads to Cinderella-like Success." *Mississippi Business Journal*, 19–25 Aug., 2002, 34.

Glaczier, Richard. "The History of Gulf Coast Hurricanes." In *Marine Resources and History of the Mississippi Gulf Coast: Mississippi's Coastal Environment*. 2 vols. Mississippi Department of Marine Resources, 1998.

Godschalk, David R., Timothy Beatley, and David J. Brower. *Catastrophic Coastal Storms*. Durham: Duke University Press, 1988.

"The Grand Isle Hurricane (1909)." *Storm Signals Online*, 25 Feb. 2002. http://www.stormsignals.com/1909.htm.

"Great Galveston Hurricane of 1900." *Storm Signals Online*, 25 Feb. 2002. http://www.stormsignals.com/1900.htm.

"Growth Accounts for Increasing Damage." *USA Today*, 17 Apr. 2000. Hurricane Information, 3 June 2002. http//:www.usatoday.com/weather/whworst.htm.

Guice, Julia. Interview by author, 30 July 2003.

Heggins, Tracy. "Out of the Rubble Emerged a Gift Shop. Storm of the Century. Hurricane Camille: 20 Years Later." Biloxi *Sun Herald*, 13 Aug. 1989, A12.

Hobbs, Mike. "Mississippi's Offshore Islands." In *Marine Resources and History of the Mississippi Gulf Coast: Mississippi's Coastal Environment*. 2 vols. Mississippi Department of Marine Resources, 1998.

"Horrific Labor Day Storm of 1935 Swept Away All But Memories." *USA Today Weather*, 8 June 1999, 3 June 2002. http://www.usatoday.com/weather/wh1935.htm.

"Hurricane Betsy." *Storm Signals Online*, 25 Feb. 2002. http://www.stormsignals.com/betsy.htm.

"Hurricane Camille." *Storm Signals Online*, 25 Feb. 2002. http://www.stormsignals.com/camille.htm.

"Hurricane Camille—Aug. 17, 1969." 1. http://www.geocities.com/hurricane/hurricanecamille.htm.

"Hurricane Camille—1969." 1. http://www.beauvoir.org/camille.html.

"Hurricane Destruction." 3 June 2002. http://www.txdirect.net/~msattler/hdestr.htm.

"Hurricane Familiarization: Destruction in a Hurricane." 9 Sept. 1998. http://www.jannws.state.ms.us/hcrn4tx.html.

"Hurricane Frederic." *Storm Signals Online*, 25 Feb. 2002. www.stormsignals.com/frederic.htm.

"Hurricane Hilda." *Storm Signals Online*, 25 Feb. 2002. http://www.stormsignals.com/hilda.htm.

"Hurricane Hunters." *FEMA for Kids: Hurricanes*, Federal Emergency Management Agency, 3 June 2002. http://www.fema.gov/kids/huhunt.htm.

"Hurricanes 1900–1999." *Extreme Weather Sourcebook 2001*, University of Colorado, 3 June 2002. http://sciencepolicy.colorado.edu/sourcebook/hurricane.html.

"Hurricanes and Societal Impacts: Are We Prepared?" *Science Now*, 5.1, fall 1997. This newsletter is a joint project of SIRS Pub., Inc., and the University Corporation for Atmospheric Research. 3 June 2002. http://www.sirs.com/corporate/newsletters/snow/snowfl97/snowfl97.htm.

Husley, Val. *Biloxi: 300 Years*. 2nd ed. Virginia Beach: The Donning Company, 1998.

Keller, Richard C. "Re: Hurricane Camille—The Richelieu." E-mail to author, 26 Mar. 2000.

"Labor Day Hurricane of 1935." *Storm Signals Online*, 25 Feb. 2002. http://www.stormsignals.com/1935.htm.

"Lack of Lights an Eerie Feeling. Hurricane Camille: 20 Years Later." Jackson *Clarion-Ledger*, 13 Aug. 1989, H1.

Lammons, George. "Storm Blew Opportunity with Disaster. Hurricane Camille: 20 Years Later." Biloxi *Sun Herald*, 20 Aug. 1989, C1.

Larson, Erick. "Waiting for Hurricane X." *Science*, 152:10. Time Magazine Archive. 7 Sept. 1998, 3 June 2002. http://www.time.com/time/magazine/1998/dom/98097/science.waiting_for_hurl5a.html.

Maines, John. "Hurricane Camille: 20 Years Later. Conditions Were Perfect in 1969 for a Killer Storm." Jackson *Clarion-Ledger*, 13 Aug. 1989, H3.

Mason, Gilbert R., with James Patterson Smith. *Beaches, Blood, and Ballots: A Black Doctor's Civil Rights Struggle*. Jackson: University Press of Mississippi, 2000.

McKenzie, Danny. "Survivor Disputes 25-Year-Old Legend of Hurricane Party." Jackson *Clarion-Ledger*, 21 Aug. 1994, B1.

McWilliams, Richebourg Gaillard, ed. *Iberville's Gulf Journals*. University, AL: University of Alabama Press, 1981.

Meadows, James. "The Barrier Islands." In *Marine Resources and His-*

tory of the Mississippi Gulf Coast: Mississippi's Coastal Environment.
2 vols. Mississippi Department of Marine Resources, 1998.

"The Mobile/Pensacola Hurricane (1906)." *Storm Signals Online*, 25
Feb. 2002. http://www.stormsignals.com/1906.htm.

Moreton, Rebecca Larche. "The French Language of the Coast." In
*Marine Resources and History of the Mississippi Gulf Coast: History,
Art, and Culture of the Mississippi Gulf Coast.* 2 vols. Mississippi
Department of Marine Resources, 1998.

"The 1915 Galveston Hurricane." *Storm Signals Online*, 25 Feb. 2002.
http://www.stormsignals.com/1915.htm.

"The 1915 New Orleans Hurricane." *Storm Signals Online*, 25 Feb. 2002.
http://www.stormsignals.com/1915new.htm.

"NOAA, NASA to Launch New Environmental Satellite." *NOAA News
Online*, 30 May 2002. National Oceanic and Atmospheric Administration, 3 June 2002. http://www.noaanews.noaa.gov/stories/
5920.htm.

"Overview of Atlantic Hurricanes: Naming Systems." 2 Feb. 2002.
http://explorezone.com/weather/hurricanes.htm.

Pender, Geoff. "Biloxi to Get Grant for Camille Museum." Biloxi *Sun
Herald*, 30 Oct. 2001.

"Perspectives on the West: Cabeza de Vaca (1490–1557)." *PBS Previews*,
Public Broadcasting System, 3 June 2002. http://www.pbs.org/weta/
thewest/people/ac/cabezadevaca.htm.

Peterson, Patrick. "Seafood Industry Suffered Several Kinds of Damage. Storm of the Century. Hurricane Camille: 20 Years Later." Biloxi
Sun Herald, 13 Aug. 1989, C1.

———. "Hurricane Season Ends; 2002 Fairly Quiet." Biloxi *Sun Herald*, 30 Nov. 2002.

Pielke, Roger A., Jr., and Roger A. Pielke, Sr. *Hurricanes: Their Nature
and Impacts on Society.* Chichester, N.Y., Weinheim, Brisbane, Singa-
pore, Toronto: John Wiley & Sons, 1997.

———. *The Hurricane.* London and New York: Routledge, 1990.

———. "What Can We Learn from Andrew?: Roger Pielke, Jr., Finds
Out." Sept. 1995. University Corporation for Atmospheric Research,
3 June 2002. http://www.ucar.edu/communications/staffnotes/
9509/pielke.htm.

Pielke, Roger A., Jr., Chantal Simonpietri, and Jennifer Oxelson.

"Twenty Years After Hurricane Camille: Lessons Learned, Lessons Lost." *Hurricane Camille: Project Report*, 12 July 1999, 6; 3 June 2002.

Powell, Murella Hebert. "Biloxi, Queen City of the Gulf Coast." In *Marine Resources and History of the Mississippi Gulf Coast: History, Art, and Culture of the Mississippi Gulf Coast.* 2 vols. Mississippi Department of Marine Resources, 1998.

―――. "The Isle of Caprice." In *Marine Resources and History of the Mississippi Gulf Coast: Mississippi's Coastal Environment.* 2 vols. Mississippi Department of Marine Resources, 1998.

Rappaport, Edward N., and Jose Fernandez. "The Deadliest Atlantic Tropical Cyclones, 1492–Present." *The National Hurricane Center.* Ed. Jack Beven, 22 Apr. 1997. National Oceanic and Atmospheric Administration, 3 June 2002. http://www.nhc.noaa.gov/pastdead/ytx.htm.

Ricketts, James. "Hurricane Camille: 20 Years Later." Jackson *Clarion-Ledger*, 13 Aug. 1989, H3.

―――. "If Camille II Hits, Gulf Coast Will be Better Prepared. Hurricane Camille: 20 Years Later." Jackson *Clarion-Ledger*, 19 Aug. 1989, 1.

Rohlfs, A. J. "Shipping and Hurricane Camille." *Mariner's Weather Log*, Nov. 1969, 248+. Weather Bureau Forecast Office, Environmental Science Services Administration, New Orleans, La. Environmental Data Service. A U.S. Department of Commerce Publication. University of Southern Mississippi Library, Vol. 13, No. 6.

Rosenfeld, Jeffrey. *Eye of the Storm: Inside the World's Deadliest Hurricanes, Tornadoes and Blizzards.* New York and London: Plenum Trade, 1999.

Ross, Frank, Jr. *Storms and Man.* New York: Lothrop, Lee and Shepard Company, 1971.

"Safety Plan Will Aid Both States." *Hattiesburg American*, 23 Oct. 2002.

"Saffir-Simpson Hurricane Scale." *The National Hurricane Center, National Oceanic and Atmospheric Administration*, 3 June 2002. http://www.nhc.noaa.gov/aboutsshs.html.

"Saffir-Simpson Scale." 9 Sept. 1998. http://mailhost.inti.net/~bsmoot/saffir.txt.

Scallan, Melissa M. "Getting the Word Out: Special Report." Biloxi *Sun Herald*, 2 Oct. 2002, B1.

Simpson, Dr. Robert H. "Tropical Storm Camille Forms Rapidly Near Grand Cayman in the Caribbean." Advisory No. 1, National Hurricane Center, Miami, 14 Aug. 1969.

Sloane, Eric. *The Book of Storms.* New York: Duell, Sloan and Pearce, 1956.

"Something to Think About." *National Oceanic and Atmospheric Administration,* 26 Feb. 2002. http://hurricanes.noaa.gov/prepare/basics_questions.htm.

Stallworth, Sharon. "Buildling Codes, Zoning Laws Rose from the Wreckage. Hurricane Camille: 20 Years Later." Biloxi *Sun Herald,* n.d., C1.

"Storms of the Century. Hurricane Camille: Part 3—Camille's Toll." *The Weather Channel/Weather Com,* 1. http//:www.weather.com/newscenter/specialreports/sotc/storm6/page3/html.

"The Story of Hurricane Camille." *The Life of Hurricane Camille,* 9 Sept. 1998. http//:www.vic.com/~mikmoody/camille.htm.

Sullivan, Charles. *Hurricanes of the Mississippi Gulf Coast.* Biloxi: Gulf Publishing Co., Inc., 1986.

Tannehill, Ivan Ray. *Hurricanes.* Princeton: Princeton University Press; London: Humphrey Milford, Oxford University Press, 1945.

Thompson, Herbert J. "The James River Flood of August 1969 in Virginia." *Weatherwise,* Office of Hydrology, ESSA-Weather Bureau, Washington, D.C., Oct. 1969, 181.

"USA's Second Straight 20th Century Hurricane." *USA Today Weather,* 7 Nov. 2000. http://www.usatoday.com/weather/wcamille.htm.

Uthoff, Christine. "Camille's Destruction Continued for Days After It Rushed Ashore." Jackson *Clarion-Ledger,* 13 Aug. 1989, H2.

"Welcome to the National Hurricane Center." *The National Hurricane Center, National Oceanic and Atmospheric Administration,* NHC Watch, 26 Feb. 2002. http://www.nhc.noaa.gov/aboutnhc.html.

"With So Much to Lose, Coast Must Not Forget Camille." Editorial, Biloxi *Sun Herald,* 13 Aug. 2000, C8.

ORAL HISTORY

Anderson, Alma. "An Oral History with Mrs. Glennan Alma Anderson." *The Mississippi Oral History Program of the University of South-*

ern Mississippi. By R. Wayne Pyle. Hattiesburg: McCain Library and Archives, Vol. 256, 1979.

DeMetz, Fred, and Dorothy Niolet. "An Oral History with Mr. Fred DeMetz and Mrs. Dorothy Niolet." *The Mississippi Oral History Program of the University of Southern Mississippi.* By R. Wayne Pyle. Hattiesburg: McCain Library and Archives, Vol. 226, 1979.

de Vries, Edith. "An Oral History with Mrs. Edith de Vries, Hurricane Camille Survivor." *The Mississippi Oral History Program of the University of Southern Mississippi.* By R. Wayne Pyle. Hattiesburg: McCain Library and Archives, Vol. 223, 1983.

Gerlach, Mary Ann. "An Oral History with Mrs. Mary Ann Gerlach, Survivor, Hurricane Camille." *The Mississippi Oral History Program of the University of Southern Mississippi.* By R. Wayne Pyle. Hattiesburg: McCain Library and Archives, Vol. 223, 1981.

Guice, Wade. "An Oral History with Mr. Wade Guice, Director, Civil Defense, Harrison County, Mississippi." *The Mississippi Oral History Program of the University of Southern Mississippi.* By R. Wayne Pyle. Hattiesburg: McCain Library and Archives, Vol. 183, 1981.

Longo, John, Jr. "An Oral History with the Honorable John Longo, Jr." *The Mississippi Oral History Program of the University of Southern Mississippi.* By R. Wayne Pyle. Hattiesburg: McCain Library and Archives, Vol. 269, 1979.

Maggio, Henry. "An Oral History with Dr. Henry Maggio, Hurricane Camille Survivor." *The Mississippi Oral History Program of the University of Southern Mississippi.* By R. Wayne Pyle. Hattiesburg: McCain Library and Archives, Vol. 240, 1980.

Merritt, Richard. "An Oral History with Mr. Richard Merritt." *The Mississippi Oral History Program of the University of Southern Mississippi.* By R. Wayne Pyle. Hattiesburg: McCain Library and Archives, Vol. 262, 1979.

Peralta, Gerald D., and Marie Peralta. "An Oral History with Gerald D. and Marie Peralta, Hurricane Camille Survivors." *The Mississippi Oral History Program of the University of Southern Mississippi.* By R. Wayne Pyle. Hattiesburg: McCain Library and Archives, Vol.224 1984.

Stegenga, Piet, and Valena Stegenga. "An Oral History with Piet and Valena Stegenga, Hurricane Camille Survivors." *The Mississippi Oral*

History Program of the University of Southern Mississippi. By R. Wayne Pyle. Hattiesburg: McCain Library and Archives, Vol 201, 1982.

Switzer, John A. "An Oral History with John A. Switzer." *The Mississippi Oral History Program of the University of Southern Mississippi.* By R. Wayne Pyle. Hattiesburg: McCain Library and Archives, Vol. 227, 1979.

Taylor, Robert Lawrence. "An Oral History with Mr. Robert Lawrence Taylor." *The Mississippi Oral History Program of the University of Southern Mississippi.* By R. Wayne Pyle. Hattiesburg: McCain Library and Archives, Vol. 275, 1979.

Toomer, Lois. "An Oral History with Mrs. Lois Toomer." *The Mississippi Oral History Program of the University of Southern Mississippi.* By R. Wayne Pyle. Hattiesburg: McCain Library and Archives, Vol. 236, 1979.

Webb, Charles. "An Oral History with Mr. Charles Webb." *The Mississippi Oral History Program of the University of Southern Mississippi.* By R. Wayne Pyle. Hattiesburg: McCain Library and Archives, Vol. 258, 1979.

Williams, Paul, Sr. "An Oral History with Mr. Paul Williams, Sr., Hurricane Camille Survivor." *The Mississippi Oral History Program of the University of Southern Mississippi.* By R. Wayne Pyle. Hattiesburg: McCain Library and Archives, Vol. 231, 1984.

INDEX

Bacall, Lauren, 66
Baldwin County, Ala., 127
Baltimore, Md., 39, 45
Baricev's Restaurant, 13, 115, 148, 184, 187
Barnes Hotel, 40
Barrett, Billy, 15, 16, 88, 94, 114, 153
Bath County, Va., 138
Baton Rouge, La., 164
Battle of Franklin (Tennessee), 44
Battle of New Orleans, 32
Bay St. Louis, Miss., 8, 10, 14, 23, 24, 30, 37, 38, 42, 48, 50, 116, 127, 128, 129, 130, 133, 135, 157, 161, 184
Bay St. Louis bridge, 117, 125
Bay St. Louis hospital, 100, 116, 156
Bayou Bernard, 31
Beach Boulevard, 117, 130
Beach Garden Society, 172
Bear Point, 39
Beatles, The, 9
Beau Rivage Casino, 188
Beaufort Scale, 79
Beaulieu, 132
Beauvoir, 41, 48, 133
Belgium, 43
Benvenutti, Elizabeth Johnson, 130
Bermuda, 60
Bielan, Mike, 27, 89, 112
Biggers, Reverend Jack, 132
Biloxi, Miss., 4, 5, 7, 8, 11, 17, 29, 31, 32, 37, 40, 42, 44, 45, 47, 48, 49, 50, 53, 55, 56, 90, 97, 98, 114, 123, 125, 129, 132, 133, 134, 149, 151, 166, 174, 176, 178, 180, 184, 187, 189, 192; airport project, 51; civil defense, 54, 93; fire of 1900, 47; police, 99; strip, 13, 54, 115, 148
Biloxi Bay, 4, 11, 23, 31, 35, 41, 46, 52, 55, 90, 93, 130
Biloxi City Cemetery, 167
Biloxi Golf Club, 50
Biloxi Holiday Inn, 162
Biloxi Indians, 29, 30, 59
Biloxi Lighthouse, 41, 43, 55, 93
Biloxi Maritime and Seafood Industry Museum, 178
Biloxi Rifles, 44
Biloxi peninsula, 33
Biloxi River, 30
Biloxi Stadium, 51
Biloxi *Sun Herald*, 126, 130, 192
Biloxi Veterans Affairs, 52
Biloxi Yacht Club, 48, 52
Biloxi-Gulfport Regional Airport, 142
Biloxi–Ocean Springs Bridge, 171
Blue Ridge Mountains, 134, 136
Bogart, Humphrey, 66
Bonnie Community, 17
Boomtown Casino, 188
Borden Milk, 140
Boston, Mass., 26, 80
Botetort County, Va., 138
Boudreaux, Ned, 181

Winn-Dixie, 174
Wittman, Mayor Joe, 172
WLOX-TV, 14, 97
Wolf River, 30
women's names, 64, 73, 74
Woodland period, 30
Woodstock Music and Art Festival, 9, 13

World Meteorological Organization, 73, 74
World War I, 49, 52, 63
World War II, 32, 52, 55, 73, 140

yellow fever, 42, 45
Yugoslavian, 38